# Twelfth Night,
# or What You Will

A Comedy by William Shakespeare

edited by Kenneth Harwood, M.A.,
English Master, Bradford Grammar School

Evans

Published by Evans Brothers Limited, Montague House,
Russell Square, London W.C.1

## Acknowledgement

The characters on the cover are taken from the Bell edition of
Shakespeare's plays, 1775-76, and represent Mr. Dodd as Mercutio,
Mr. Macklin as Shylock, Mr. Lewis as Prince Hal, (back), Mr.
King as Touchstone, Mr. Garrick as Macbeth and Mrs. Mattocks
as Katharine, (front).

They are reproduced by kind permission of the Harry R.
Beard Theatre Collection.

Printed in Great Britain by T. & A. Constable Ltd., Edinburgh

237   28548   7                                          PR 1409

# The Montague Shakespeare

The intention of the editors has been to make the plays completely intelligible to twentieth-century readers without falsifying the originals.

The Text departs from custom in two major respects:

1   We count each line of print as a line, ignoring whether it is only part of a line of verse: thus when a verse line is shared by two speakers, it counts as two. This makes for ease of reference.

To be logical, and again for ease of reference, we have also counted overflowing lines as two.

We have divided some long speeches into paragraphs, as would be normal in any other kind of writing. This is designed to help readers to see the movement of thought through a speech.

2   We have tried to adopt a completely modern system of punctuation and spelling; we have thus expanded such puzzling spellings as *i' th' garden* and *i' faith*. Teachers will remember many unwanted laughs caused by such relics of the past.

The Notes are directed primarily towards explaining the plain meaning of Shakespeare's words. This is done in two ways: by giving short verbal equivalents where the general sense is clear, and by giving more extended paraphrase where the thought remains difficult even when the individual words may be explained. A third type of note, printed in *italics*, is meant to provide a running commentary on the action and motives, so that the reader does not miss the dramatic significance of what he is reading.

In basing the Montague Shakespeare on the First Folio of 1623, we have kept some of the lineation of the original in disputed places; but we have accepted, as all editors indeed must, many emendations of the past 350 years. We think we have explained everything that we print, and in this franker age present a much less bowdlerised text than the normal school edition.

K.H.G.

# Twelfth Night

To us nowadays, January 6th, twelve days after Christmas, means little more than a rather drab day when, by tradition, the Christmas decorations, cards and tree are taken down, and our houses, shops and streets suddenly seem very ordinary again. To the Elizabethans, however, January 6th was the spectacular and popular festival of Twelfth Night. As the climax to the holiday revels, it was an occasion when the authorities allowed their servants to do pretty well what they pleased—hence the play's subtitle, *What You Will*.

Shakespeare's play, written in 1600, may well have had its first performance on Twelfth Night, 1601. On that night the queen was entertaining various English and foreign noblemen, including an Italian duke called Virginio Orsino, and a play which may have been this one was part of the entertainment in the great hall at Whitehall Palace.

Whether or not Shakespeare had this particular occasion in mind, the play reflects clearly the spirit of this festivity. It ridicules those in authority—Malvolio, Orsino and Olivia come in for varying degrees of ridicule—while it allows free scope to the lawlessness of Sir Toby and the mockery of Feste.

Feste, Sir Toby, Sir Andrew and Malvolio, and the part of the story that is woven round them, are all inventions of Shakespeare. The basic story of the separated twins, Viola and Sebastian, and their romantic adventures in the country of Orsino and Olivia, is an old one that Shakespeare could have come across in one of several versions. A plot which grows into a tangle of love-affairs, made all the more confusing by the heroine's disguising herself as a boy, would be one to appeal to Shakespeare at this period of his play-writing, when within the last two years he had written plays such as *As You Like It* and *Much Ado About Nothing*, which with this play are usually grouped together and labelled 'romantic comedies'.

A label such as this is not always very helpful. Compared with modern plays, this may seem rather different from our ideas of romance; but as to its being a comedy, there can be no doubt. It is comedy in a wide range of forms: slapstick, topical satire, mistaken identity, juggling with words, comic situations, etc. How does it manage to combine all these ingredients? This is a question best left unanswered—for we rarely appreciate a joke if it has to be explained laboriously to us. The only answer is to read the play and see it as often as possible—and each time something new will be found in it.

# List of Characters

| | |
|---|---|
| ORSINO | Duke of Illyria |
| SEBASTIAN | a gentleman from Messaline |
| SIR TOBY BELCH | Olivia's uncle |
| SIR ANDREW AGUECHEEK | a friend of Sir Toby |
| ANTONIO | a sea-captain and friend of Sebastian |
| CURIO<br>VALENTINE | } gentlemen attendants of Orsino |
| MALVOLIO | Olivia's steward |
| FABIAN | a servant of Olivia |
| FESTE | Olivia's family jester |
| OLIVIA | a countess and wealthy heiress |
| VIOLA | who uses the name of Cesario; Sebastian's sister |
| MARIA | Olivia's lady-in-waiting |
| A Sea-Captain | of Illyria |
| A Priest | |
| Two Officers | of the law |
| A Servant | of Olivia |

Attendants (of Orsino and Olivia), sailors, musicians

Illyria, where all the action happens, gives the story a sense of remoteness—any surprise or coincidence is possible there. A young elegant nobleman listens attentively to his small group of court musicians playing a richly romantic tune. Gradually, we see that he is deliberately posing as a distressed lover. His exaggeratedly sentimental language gives away Orsino's weakness, that he is in a sense enjoying himself in this role.

1-3    'If, as they say, love is stimulated by music, then keep on playing, so that my love like any ordinary appetite becomes so full to overflowing that it ceases to want any more.'

4    *Orsino asks for the last few bars to be played again. The sweeping descent from high to low notes*, 'a dying fall', *has fitted in exactly with his melancholy mood like a great sigh. A sigh makes him think of the* 'sweet sound' *of the breeze as it brushes over a patch of violets.*

7    'Carrying away the scent of the violets, and then blowing back over the same spot still carrying the heavy scent'

10-16    'What an incredible thing love is! It's so active and greedy that it gets things out of all proportion. It's like the sea in the sense that it can consume anything. It doesn't matter how great and important something is—as soon as you are in love it immediately becomes of no importance at all. A lover lives so completely in the world of his imagination, that no other ideas can be half as fanciful as his.'

13    **pitch :** high value (*literally: the height to which a falcon soars*)

17    *Curio suggests a distraction, but it is no use—Orsino can think of only one thing: his* 'hunting' *for Olivia's heart.*

20-25    'That's exactly what I am doing: I am hot on the chase of the most desirable heart in the dukedom. When I first saw Olivia, she looked so sweet that I thought her presence would be enough to purify the air of any plague germs. At that very moment I ceased to be the one doing the chasing and became like a stag chased by menacing and vicious dogs; in my case it was love that was after me, as it has been ever since.' (*Orsino is comparing himself to the hunter Actaeon who was punished by the goddess Diana for seeing her bathing. He was turned into a stag and chased and torn to pieces by his own hounds.*)

# ACT 1

SCENE 1   Orsino's palace in Illyria

*Enter* Duke, Curio, *lords and musicians.*

Duke If music be the food of love, play on;
Give me excess of it; that, surfeiting,
The appetite may sicken, and so die.
 That strain again—it had a dying fall;
O, it came o'er my ear, like the sweet sound
That breathes upon a bank of violets,
Stealing and giving odour.
 Enough, no more!
'Tis not so sweet now as it was before.
 O spirit of love, how quick and fresh art thou, 10
That, notwithstanding thy capacity
Receiveth as the sea, nought enters there,
Of what validity and pitch soe'er,
But falls into abatement and low price
Even in a minute; so full of shapes is fancy,
That it alone is high fantastical.

Curio Will you go hunt, my lord?

Duke What, Curio?

Curio The hart.

Duke Why, so I do, the noblest that I have. 20
O, when mine eyes did see Olivia first,
Methought she purged the air of pestilence;
That instant was I turned into a hart,
And my desires, like fell and cruel hounds,
E'er since pursue me.

*Enter* Valentine

How now, what news from her?

| 27–35 | 'I'm sorry, my lord, but I wasn't able to see her; all I got was this answer from her maid-servant: she won't show her face fully to the world for seven years; instead she will wear a veil like a nun and regularly weep in her room once a day. She will do all this to preserve her love for her dead brother so that he doesn't fade away in her memory.' (*Olivia's message, which Valentine quotes, is phrased in exactly the same extravagant language as Orsino uses. When its meaning is simplified, the audience can see what a ridiculously excessive show of sorrow Olivia has vowed for herself.*) |

| 29 | **The element:** the sky |

| 33 | **eye-offending brine:** salt tears which trouble her eyes (*The mention of* 'salt' *leads to the fanciful metaphor of using her tears to* 'season' *and* 'keep fresh' *her love, like salt preserving meat.*) |

| 36–43 | 'Just think! If Olivia's heart is so sensitive that she can so dutifully love a mere brother, what devoted love she must be capable of when Cupid's arrow of love has driven from her heart the hundred and one trifling feelings she may have for other people and planted there one man to rule over all the thoughts and feelings that make her the perfect goddess!' |

| 40 | **liver, brain and heart:** *From these three parts of the body Elizabethans believed that passions, reason and sentiments respectively originated. These were the vital controlling parts of the body.* |

| 44–46 | *Orsino has rejected the suggestion to go hunting. Instead, he will lie in his garden among the flowers, trusting that the scent will further stimulate his thoughts of love.* |

| 45–46 | **canopied with bowers:** screened by the branches |

## Scene 2

A teenage girl, clothes drenched by the sea, accompanied by a few humble sailors who have all just stumbled out of the sea after saving her, is quite a contrast to Orsino in the idle splendour of his court. She is like Olivia in having, as far as she knows, lost her brother, but her reaction to this loss is far more practical.

| 4 | **Elysium:** heaven (*the word would sound very like* 'Illyria') |
| 5 | **perchance:** perhaps (*Viola is optimistic by nature*) |

| Val. | So please my lord, I might not be admitted, |
| | But from her handmaid do return this answer: |
| | The element itself, till seven years' heat, |
| | Shall not behold her face at ample view; 30 |
| | But, like a cloistress, she will veiled walk, |
| | And water once a day her chamber round |
| | With eye-offending brine; all this to season |
| | A brother's dead love, which she would keep fresh |
| | And lasting in her sad remembrance. |
| Duke | O she that hath a heart of that fine frame |
| | To pay this debt of love but to a brother, |
| | How will she love, when the rich golden shaft |
| | Hath killed the flock of all affections else |
| | That live in her; when liver, brain and heart, 40 |
| | These sovereign thrones, are all supplied, and filled |
| | Her sweet perfections with one self king! |
| | Away before me to sweet beds of flowers; |
| | Love-thoughts lie rich when canopied with bowers. |

*Exeunt*


SCENE 2   Near the sea-coast of Illyria
*Enter* Viola, *a* Captain *and sailors.*

| Viola | What country, friends, is this? |
| Captain | This is Illyria, lady. |
| Viola | And what should I do in Illyria? |
| | My brother he is in Elysium. |
| | Perchance he is not drowned. What think you, sailors? |
| Captain | It is perchance that you yourself were saved. |

7, 8    **perchance:** by chance

10–21    *The Captain's speech acts like a film flash-back to recall the recent shipwreck, the few survivors in the drifting—'driving'—boat, and the heroic idea of Viola's brother fighting the sea as he clung to the floating mast.*

14–21    'I saw your brother taking the wisest course in such a danger and lashing himself—he was so brave and certain of himself that he saw what was the best thing to do—to a strong mast floating safely on the waves. There I saw him—just like that Greek poet Arion who used a dolphin's back to carry him safely to the shore—battling it out strongly with the waves all the while he remained in sight.'

23–25    'The fact that I was lucky enough to survive, together with what you have just said, makes me hopeful that he will survive too.'

29    *The Captain is a simple, unaffected man, and so the audience readily accepts what he says about Orsino and Olivia. If the first scene has shown Orsino in a poor light, these words will help to restore the idea of Orsino as an attractive young man who would at once make a girl of Viola's age curious to meet him.*

36    'the report was just being put about'

37    **the less:** ordinary folk (*This explains how the Captain knows the court gossip. The audience is given the relevant facts about Olivia before she appears.*)

39    'Who is she?'

| | |
|---|---|
| Viola | O, my poor brother! And so perchance may he be. |
| Captain | True, madam, and to comfort you with chance,   10<br>Assure yourself, after our ship did split,<br>When you and those poor number saved with you<br>Hung on our driving boat, I saw your brother,<br>Most provident in peril, bind himself—<br>Courage and hope both teaching him the practice—<br>To a strong mast that lived upon the sea;<br>Where, like Arion on the dolphin's back,<br>I saw him hold acquaintance with the waves   20<br>So long as I could see. |
| Viola | For saying so, there's gold.<br>Mine own escape unfoldeth to my hope,<br>Whereto thy speech serves for authority,<br>The like of him. Knowest thou this country? |
| Captain | Ay, madam, well, for I was bred and born<br>Not three hours' travel from this very place. |
| Viola | Who governs here? |
| Captain | A noble duke, in nature as in name. |
| Viola | What is his name?   30 |
| Captain | Orsino. |
| Viola | Orsino! I have heard my father name him.<br>He was a bachelor then. |
| Captain | And so is now, or was so very late;<br>For but a month ago I went from hence,<br>And then 'twas fresh in murmur—as you know<br>What great ones do the less will prattle of—<br>That he did seek the love of fair Olivia. |
| Viola | What's she? |

| | |
|---|---|
| 45 | **abjured:** sworn to avoid |
| 47–50 | 'I wish I were able to get a job with her. Then I could wait for the right moment to tell everyone who I am and what my rank is in society.' (*Viola is a wealthy girl shipwrecked in a strange country. She naturally is cautious about throwing herself at the mercy of strangers until she has a good look at the country's rulers.*) |
| 51 | **compass:** arrange |
| 52 | **suit:** request (*in Viola's case*); courting (*in Orsino's case*) |
| 54–58 | 'Captain, I feel I can trust you. I know that nature has so arranged things that often beauty is a cover for an evil mind, but in your case I am ready to believe that you are as honest and open as you appear.' (*In the play many of the characters let themselves be deluded by appearances. Viola is one of the exceptions. In this case she is prepared to trust the Captain, but she shows that she is well aware of the need for caution.*) |
| 57 | **suits:** corresponds |
| 60 | **me:** for my sake |
| 60–62 | **be my aid . . . intent:** 'help me to get hold of a disguise which will do for what I have in mind' |
| 63 | **eunuch:** the sort of male servant found at the courts of sultans and other Eastern princes |
| 64 | *She promises to make it worth the Captain's trouble; she still has some money saved from the shipwreck, as line 22 shows.* |
| 65 | **speak:** play |
| 66 | **allow:** prove |
| 66 | *Shakespeare is giving the audience a reason why Viola should so quickly be taken into and promoted in Orsino's service. Her musical talents are not shown in the play, but they would be a useful recommendation to a duke who relies so much on the moody quality of music.* |
| 67 | *Viola is an optimist, prepared to leave the rest to luck.* |
| 68 | 'All you have to do in this affair is to keep your mouth shut.' |
| 68 | **wit:** plan |
| 69–71 | *The Captain agrees to keep Viola's secret, though he exaggerates to show his willingness.* |
| 69 | **mute:** a servant whose tongue had been removed to make him keep his master's secrets |
| 70–71 | 'If I give you away, then you can put out my eyes to punish me.' |

| | | |
|---|---|---|
| Captain | A virtuous maid, the daughter of a count | 40 |
| | That died some twelvemonth since, then leaving her | |
| | In the protection of his son, her brother, | |
| | Who shortly also died; for whose dear love, | |
| | They say, she hath abjured the sight | |
| | And company of men. | |
| Viola | O that I served that lady, | |
| | And might not be delivered to the world, | |
| | Till I had made mine own occasion mellow, | |
| | What my estate is! | 50 |
| Captain | That were hard to compass, | |
| | Because she will admit no kind of suit; | |
| | No, not the duke's. | |
| Viola | There is a fair behaviour in thee, captain; | |
| | And though that nature with a beauteous wall | |
| | Doth oft close in pollution, yet of thee | |
| | I will believe thou hast a mind that suits | |
| | With this thy fair and outward character. | |
| | I prithee—and I'll pay thee bounteously— | |
| | Conceal me what I am, and be my aid | 60 |
| | For such disguise as haply shall become | |
| | The form of my intent. I'll serve this duke; | |
| | Thou shalt present me as an eunuch to him— | |
| | It may be worth thy pains—for I can sing | |
| | And speak to him in many sorts of music, | |
| | That will allow me very worth his service. | |
| | What else may hap to time I will commit; | |
| | Only shape thou thy silence to my wit. | |
| Captain | Be you his eunuch, and your mute I'll be, | |
| | When my tongue blabs, then let mine eyes not see! | 70 |
| Viola | I thank thee. Lead me on. *Exeunt* | |

Prose, clowning and coarse good humour completely change the atmosphere and speed of the play. The audience is surprised to find that such a non-tragic figure as Sir Toby is Olivia's uncle. There is none of the melancholy atmosphere as Maria pursues Sir Toby scolding him for returning late from one of his drinking sessions. Sir Toby's bellowed first speech, in defence of a life free from care, is the first of a series of challenges to the sort of behaviour to which Olivia has apparently dedicated herself.

4–6    *Maria clearly shows that Olivia is mistress of the household.*

5    **cousin:** a vague term, which could refer to any relation

7    'Then let her make an exception of anyone like me whom she has already made an exception of.' (*Sir Toby is often comical in the way he prides himself on being quick-witted. He loves a play on words, as here where he twists a legal phrase to apply to himself.*)

8–9    'Yes, but you must restrain yourself a bit; you have to stay inside the bounds of what's right and proper.' (*Sir Toby deliberately misunderstands the word* 'confine' *and pretends Maria is criticising his clothes which are not his* 'finest'. *It is an easier charge for him to answer.*)

12    **an:** if

14    **That . . . you:** 'Your hitting the bottle and constant drinking will be the end of you.' (*Sir Toby has to watch his step; there is always a chance that Olivia will throw him out of her house.*)

17    *Since Olivia has taken this seven-year vow, it seems a fantastic idea that Sir Andrew should be* 'her wooer' *and hope to marry her. The idea grows more fantastic as the picture of this foolish gentleman develops.*

18    **Aguecheek:** the name suggests a pale thin face, as of someone suffering from a gnawing pain

20    'He's as dashing as anyone you're likely to find in this country.'

22    *Sir Andrew's income (about £1000 a year and now worth far more) is Sir Toby's real interest in him.*

23–24    'Yes, but he won't have all that for more than a year; he's nothing but a silly spendthrift.'

25    **Fie . . . so:** 'Shame on you for saying so!'

25–26    **viol-de-gamboys:** an Elizabethan stringed instrument, something between a violin and a 'cello

SCENE 3   Olivia's house in Illyria
*Enter* Sir Toby *and* Maria.

Toby     What a plague means my niece to take the death
         of her brother thus? I am sure care's an enemy to
         life.

Maria    By my troth, Sir Toby, you must come in earlier
         o' nights; your cousin, my lady, takes great
         exceptions to your ill hours.

Toby     Why, let her except before excepted.

Maria    Ay, but you must confine yourself within the
         modest limits of order.

Toby     Confine! I'll confine myself no finer than I am.   10
         These clothes are good enough to drink in, and so
         be these boots too; an they be not, let them hang
         themselves in their own straps.

Maria    That quaffing and drinking will undo you. I
         heard my lady talk of it yesterday, and of a
         foolish knight that you brought in one night here
         to be her wooer.

Toby     Who, Sir Andrew Aguecheek?

Maria    Ay, he.

Toby     He's as tall a man as any's in Illyria.            20

Maria    What's that to the purpose?

Toby     Why, he has three thousand ducats a year.

Maria    Ay, but he'll have but a year in all these ducats.
         He's a very fool and a prodigal.

Toby     Fie, that you'll say so! He plays on the viol-de-
         gamboys, and speaks three or four languages
         word for word without book, and hath all the
         good gifts of nature.

29 **natural:** to call a man 'a natural' was as much as to say 'a born idiot'

30–34 **and but . . . grave:** 'and if he weren't so much of a coward, which helps to cancel out his passion for quarrelling, then anyone with any sense could see that he would very soon get himself killed' (*To be able to quarrel according to an elaborately organised method was considered part of a gentleman's accomplishments. Sir Andrew tries hard to imitate gentlemen.*)

35–36 **substractors:** *Sir Toby drunkenly stumbles for the word 'detractors', meaning 'slanderers'.*

37–38 *A sly way of returning the subject to Sir Toby's own folly.*

41 **coystrill:** rogue

42–43 **till . . . toe:** 'until his head is reeling'

43 **parish-top:** a giant-size top, owned by a parish, and available for any villager to play with

44–45 **Castiliano . . . Agueface:** *Sir Toby is fond of trying to impress others by knowing snatches of foreign languages. His Spanish does not mean much now, but, like his deliberate mistaking of Sir Andrew's name, is meant to be impolite.*

46 *The first mention of Sir Toby's full name; its repetition ensures that the audience sees how appropriate the surname is.*

48 **fair shrew:** *Sir Andrew is trying hard to be gallant, but innocently chooses the wrong word. A 'shrew' suggests a cross or nagging woman.*

50 *Sir Toby is really saying something like: 'Go on, give her a kiss', but the word 'accost' baffles Sir Andrew, who thinks it is her name.*

57 **front her:** go up to her
**board her:** take hold of her

| | |
|---|---|
| Maria | He hath indeed—almost natural. For besides that he's a fool, he's a great quarreller; and but that 30 he hath the gift of a coward to allay the gust he hath in quarrelling, 'tis thought among the prudent he would quickly have the gift of a grave. |
| Toby | By this hand, they are scoundrels and sub-stractors that say so of him. Who are they? |
| Maria | They that add, moreover, he's drunk nightly in your company. |
| Toby | With drinking healths to my niece. I'll drink to her as long as there is a passage in my throat and 40 drink in Illyria. He's a coward and a coystrill that will not drink to my niece till his brains turn on the toe, like a parish-top. What, wench! Castiliano vulgo! For here comes Sir Andrew Agueface. |

*Enter* Sir Andrew

| | |
|---|---|
| Andrew | Sir Toby Belch! How now, Sir Toby Belch? |
| Toby | Sweet Sir Andrew! |
| Andrew | Bless you, fair shrew. |
| Maria | And you too, sir. |
| Toby | Accost, Sir Andrew, accost. 50 |
| Andrew | What's that? |
| Toby | My niece's chambermaid. |
| Andrew | Good Mistress Accost, I desire better acquaintance. |
| Maria | My name is Mary, sir. |
| Andrew | Good Mistress Mary Accost— |
| Toby | You mistake, knight; 'accost' is front her, board her, woo her, assail her. |

59–60   **undertake ... company:** 'take her on, with people watching'
(*Sir Toby, for a laugh, is urging his friend to practise being a
gentleman courting a lady, but Sir Andrew is too shy and embarrassed
to perform in public.*)

62–63   'If you let her go now, Sir Andrew, then you can never again
call yourself a man.' (*Rather pathetically, Sir Andrew can only
repeat the phrase after his tutor. When he tries a phrase of his own,
it needs so little twisting by Maria to make him seem a complete
fool.*)

66   **in hand:** to deal with

68   *Sir Andrew innocently thinks Maria is encouraging his attentions.*

69   **thought is free:** a proverbial saying, meaning: 'I can think
what I like—but you'll never know' (*Now that she is holding
his hand she can answer his question as to what she thinks—line 65.*)

69–70   **I pray ... drink:** *Maria uses a serving-girl's way of asking for
a kiss and some reward, but again Sir Andrew does not understand.*

71   **What's your metaphor?:** I don't follow you

72   'It's fallen flat.' (*because Sir Andrew has not understood her*); and
'It's just your meanness.' (*to have a 'dry' hand was supposed to
be a sign of miserliness with money and in love. To Sir Andrew, the
word 'dry' has only its ordinary meaning.*)

75   **dry:** stupid

77   **at my fingers' ends:** where her hand is touching Sir
Andrew's (*She is saying that he is a source of endless jokes to her.
With him gone, she has nothing to laugh at—she is 'barren'.*)

79–80   'Come on now, Sir Andrew; you could do with a drink. I've
never seen you made such a fool of, have I?'

82   **put me down:** knock me out (*by making him drunk*) (*Sir
Andrew makes the pun rather sadly. He has to agree that he has no
exceptional amount of intelligence—'wit'—though he comes out with
the common explanation that eating beef was supposed to dull one's
brain.*)

86   'There's no doubt about that.' (*Sir Toby's heavy sarcasm is
enough to make Sir Andrew despair of his hopes of marrying Olivia.
His departure is the last thing that Sir Toby wants, so he has to
keep turning the conversation in other directions.*)

87   **forswear it:** give up eating beef

| | |
|---|---|
| Andrew | By my troth, I would not undertake her in this company. Is that the meaning of 'accost'? 60 |
| Maria | Fare you well, gentlemen. |
| Toby | An thou let her part so, Sir Andrew, would thou mightest never draw sword again! |
| Andrew | An you part so, mistress, I would I might never draw sword again! Fair lady, do you think you have fools in hand? |
| Maria | Sir, I have not you by the hand. |
| Andrew | Marry, but you shall have, and here's my hand. |
| Maria | Now, sir, thought is free. I pray you, bring your hand to the buttery-bar and let it drink. 70 |
| Andrew | Wherefore, sweetheart? What's your metaphor? |
| Maria | It's dry, sir. |
| Andrew | Why, I think so; I am not such an ass but I can keep my hand dry. But what's your jest? |
| Maria | A dry jest, sir. |
| Andrew | Are you full of them? |
| Maria | Ay, sir, I have them at my fingers' ends; marry, now I let go your hand, I am barren. |

*Exit*

| | |
|---|---|
| Toby | O knight, thou lackest a cup of canary. When did I see thee so put down? 80 |
| Andrew | Never in your life, I think, unless you see canary put me down. Methinks, sometimes, I have no more wit than a Christian or an ordinary man has—but I am a great eater of beef, and I believe that does harm to my wit. |
| Toby | No question! |
| Andrew | An I thought that, I'd forswear it. I'll ride home tomorrow, Sir Toby. |

89     **Pourquoi:** *One French word is enough to show that Sir Andrew is not the linguist Sir Toby claimed in line 26.*

91     **bestowed . . . tongues:** 'spent that time learning foreign languages' (*Sir Toby pretends he would like to have spent the time with his hair in curling tongs—pronounced 'tongues'.*)

94–101     *The insults about Sir Andrew's thin lank hair are Sir Toby's coarse way of saying Sir Andrew is only half a man. They also give a clear idea of his appearance on the stage.*

99     **flax on a distaff:** fibres of flax hanging loosely on a stick ready to be spun to make linen

100     **housewife:** woman (*Sir Andrew does not notice the strong sexual suggestion in this speech.*)

104–105     **hard by:** a near neighbour

106–108     'She won't have anything to do with the Count. She won't agree to marry anyone she thinks is above her—whether he's better off than she is, or older, or more intelligent; I've heard her swear that she won't. Cheer up, there's hope for you yet, man.' (*If this is true, it partly explains why, later, Olivia is so ready to consider marrying a messenger.*)

109–111     **I am . . . altogether:** 'You know, I'm the strangest fellow imaginable; sometimes there's nothing I like better than acting and singing and dancing about.'

110     **masques:** a popular court entertainment—a mixture of acting, singing, and dressing up

111     **revels:** organised frolics at court (*Masques and revels were particularly popular at Twelfth Night.*)

112     **kickchawses:** fancy tricks

113–115     'I'm as good as anyone you could mention in Illyria— although I'd not compare myself with my social superiors, nor with a more experienced man.' (*Sir Andrew quickly moderates his boast. The 'older', more experienced, man may well be Sir Toby who is prancing about the stage as well as drink will allow him. From this point on, Sir Andrew leaps and high-kicks grotesquely to the amusement of his friend.*)

116     'What part of the galliard do you specialise in?' (*The 'galliard' was a lively dance which included some leaps in the air—*'capers'.)

118     *Sir Toby pretends that Sir Andrew has said that he can cut up the herb, 'caper', to make the sauce which was served with mutton.*

119     **back-trick:** *Sir Andrew, like the 'stooge' in a pair of comedians, ignores or fails to understand Sir Toby's jests, and persists in demonstrating his dancing—this time an acrobatic leap backwards.*

| | |
|---|---|
| Toby | Pourquoi, my dear knight? |
| Andrew | What is 'pourquoi'? Do or not do? I would I had 90 bestowed that time in the tongues that I have in fencing, dancing and bear-baiting; O, had I but followed the arts! |
| Toby | Then hadst thou had an excellent head of hair. |
| Andrew | Why, would that have mended my hair? |
| Toby | Past question, for thou seest it will not curl by nature. |
| Andrew | But it becomes me well enough, does it not? |
| Toby | Excellent; it hangs like flax on a distaff, and I hope to see a housewife take thee between her legs 100 and spin it off. |
| Andrew | Faith, I'll home tomorrow, Sir Toby. Your niece will not be seen; or, if she be, it's four to one she'll none of me. The count himself here hard by woos her. |
| Toby | She'll none of the count—she'll not match above her degree, neither in estate, years nor wit; I have heard her swear it. Tut, there's life in it, man. |
| Andrew | I'll stay a month longer. I am a fellow of the strangest mind in the world—I delight in masques 110 and revels sometimes altogether. |
| Toby | Art thou good at these kickchawses, knight? |
| Andrew | As any man in Illyria, whatsoever he be, under the degree of my betters; and yet I will not compare with an old man. |
| Toby | What is thy excellence in a galliard, knight? |
| Andrew | Faith, I can cut a caper. |
| Toby | And I can cut the mutton to it. |
| Andrew | And I think I have the back-trick simply as strong as any man in Illyria. 120 |

125–127    **coranto, jig, sink-a-pace:** all names of lively dances, like the galliard (*Sir Toby mockingly insists that Sir Andrew should display his dancing talent at all times, performing one dance on the way to church, and another on the return, etc. He should not neglect his skill, to let it collect dust like portraits of Mistress Mall, which would be hidden behind a curtain. This is probably a reference to the court beauty, Mary Fitton, who had recently been disgraced.*)

128–130    **I did . . . galliard:** 'By the look of your shapely legs, I was sure you must have been born under a dancing star.' (*Sir Andrew's legs are like broomsticks—hence Sir Toby's sarcasm.*)

131–132    **Ay . . . stock:** 'Yes, it is rather a fine leg, and it doesn't look at all bad in bright orange stockings.' (*The colour would exaggerate Sir Andrew's skinniness.*)

134–135    **born under Taurus:** *The old belief was that a person's character was affected by the situation of the stars when he was born. Sir Toby corrects Sir Andrew's astrology, trying to persuade him that he is a born dancer because he was born in the sign of the zodiac, Taurus.*

137    *The scene ends with both knights capering delightedly off stage, Olivia and Maria's warning completely forgotten for the moment.*

| Toby | Wherefore are these things hid? Wherefore have these gifts a curtain before them? Are they like to take dust, like Mistress Mall's picture? Why dost thou not go to church in a galliard, and come home in a coranto? My very walk should be a jig. I would not so much as make water but in a sink-a-pace. What dost thou mean? Is it a world to hide virtues in? I did think, by the excellent constitution of thy leg, it was formed under the star of a galliard. 130 |
|---|---|
| Andrew | Ay, 'tis strong, and it does indifferent well in a flame-coloured stock. Shall we set about some revels? |
| Toby | What shall we do else? Were we not born under Taurus? |
| Andrew | Taurus? That's sides and heart. |
| Toby | No, sir, it is legs and thighs. Let me see thee caper. Ha, higher! Ha, ha, excellent! |

*Exeunt*

Viola's next appearance is to be as special envoy between the two courts. This scene shows how she comes to be chosen and explains the secret difficulties caused by her disguise. Viola and Valentine enter, apparently in the middle of a conversation.

2     **Cesario:** *The audience must know Viola's new name as soon as possible.*

        **like . . . advanced:** likely to be promoted considerably

3     **but three days:** *In the play, people fall in or out of love almost at a glance, but, not to stretch belief too far, Viola is given three days in which to impress and fall in love with Orsino.*

5-7    'If you doubt whether Orsino will continue to favour me, you must think either that he is a changeable sort of man, or that I shall suddenly stop trying to please him.'

10    *Orsino's immediate singling out of Cesario shows how important the new servant has become to his master.*

11    'He is here waiting your command, my lord.'

12    **aloof:** out of the way (*Orsino's instructions to Cesario are typical of a lover concerned only with the importance of his own passion. Viola's brief replies and practical objections to the scheme reveal a far cooler mind.*)

13-19   'Cesario, you know all the details of this business; I've told you all my secret thoughts. So, be a good fellow and go to her; don't let them keep you out; stay there outside her gate and tell them you'll stay there until they let you in to see her, even if you have to take root on the spot.'

23-24   'Demand admittance; be rude if necessary—that's better than coming back empty-handed.'

26-30   'Then it's your chance to tell her all about my deep love for her. Overwhelm her with your account of how faithfully I worship her—you should be the right man for demonstrating to her the agonies I am enduring. She will listen to it better coming from a young man than if it came from a messenger who was older and more serious.' (*Orsino uses all the phrases of a suffering lover, believing that if only Olivia knew of his suffering she would at once return his love. This and the next speech show why Orsino has chosen Cesario as his envoy.*)

SCENE 4  Orsino's palace

*Enter* Valentine, *and* Viola *dressed as a man.*

Val.    If the duke continue these favours towards you,
        Cesario, you are like to be much advanced; he
        hath known you but three days, and already you
        are no stranger.

Viola   You either fear his humour or my negligence,
        that you call in question the continuance of his
        love. Is he inconstant, sir, in his favours?

Val.    No, believe me.

Viola   I thank you. Here comes the count.

        *Enter* Duke, Curio *and attendants*

Duke    Who saw Cesario, ho?                                    10

Viola   On your attendance, my lord, here.

Duke    (*to all but* Viola) Stand you awhile aloof.
            Cesario,
        Thou knowest no less, but all; I have unclasped
        To thee the book even of my secret soul.
        Therefore, good youth, address thy gait unto her;
        Be not denied access, stand at her doors,
        And tell them there thy fixed foot shall grow
        Till thou have audience.

Viola   Sure, my noble lord,                                    20
        If she be so abandoned to her sorrow
        As it is spoke, she never will admit me.

Duke    Be clamorous and leap all civil bounds
        Rather than make unprofited return.

Viola   Say I do speak with her, my lord, what then?

Duke    O, then unfold the passion of my love,
        Surprise her with discourse of my dear faith—

33–39   'Anyone who calls you a man will be making you out to be older than you look. The lips of the goddess Diana could not be more smooth or ruby-red than yours, and your light voice is high-pitched and musical like a girl's; you are just like a woman in all these ways. I can see that the stars have designed you from birth to be exactly the man to handle this situation.'

41–42   **for I . . . company:** 'for I am better off alone'

46–47   'Yet how difficult the job is going to be! No matter who it is that I court on Orsino's behalf, I shall be wishing myself in her position.' (*Viola has no one to whom she can confide her secret love for Orsino, but the audience needs to know of it at this stage, so that the difficulty of her mission to her rival, Olivia, can be fully understood in the next act.*)

## Scene 5

Olivia has been constantly in the minds of the other characters so far; now at last she appears, to dominate this her only scene in the first two acts. While the audience await Viola's arrival, they are shown Olivia's queen-like control over her household. A paid jester seems as out-of-keeping as Sir Toby in a house of mourning.

3   *Maria reminds us that Feste's position is perilous—an unfortunate remark might lose him his job or his life. Where he has been is never made clear. The important point is that he starts the play out of favour with the authorities—Olivia and Malvolio.*

5   *The jester's chief asset is his quick wit for twisting the meaning of words. Here Feste is punning on the word* 'colours', *pronounced* 'collars'—*halters for hanging people.*

6   **colours:** enemy (who could be recognised by their standards —'colours')

|         |                                                      |    |
|---------|------------------------------------------------------|----|
|         | It shall become thee well to act my woes;            |    |
|         | She will attend it better in thy youth,              |    |
|         | Than in a nuncio's of more grave aspect.             | 30 |
| Viola   | I think not so, my lord.                              |    |
| Duke    | Dear lad, believe it.                                 |    |
|         | For they shall yet belie thy happy years,            |    |
|         | That say thou art a man. Diana's lip                 |    |
|         | Is not more smooth and rubious; thy small pipe       |    |
|         | Is as the maiden's organ, shrill and sound;          |    |
|         | And all is semblative a woman's part.                |    |
|         | I know thy constellation is right apt                |    |
|         | For this affair.                                      |    |
|         | Some four or five attend him—                        | 40 |
|         | All, if you will; for I myself am best               |    |
|         | When least in company. Prosper well in this,         |    |
|         | And thou shalt live as freely as thy lord,           |    |
|         | To call his fortunes thine.                           |    |
| Viola   | I'll do my best                                       |    |
|         | To woo your lady. (aside) Yet a barful strife!       |    |
|         | Whoe'er I woo, myself would be his wife.              |    |

*Exeunt*

SCENE 5   Olivia's house
*Enter* Maria *and* Feste.

| Maria   | Nay, either tell me where thou hast been, or I will  |
|         | not open my lips so wide as a bristle may enter, in  |
|         | way of thy excuse. My lady will hang thee for thy    |
|         | absence.                                             |
| Feste   | Let her hang me. He that is well hanged in this      |
|         | world needs to fear no colours.                      |

7   'Prove it.'

8   *Feste means that if he is hanged he will be past seeing or fearing any enemy.*

9-10   'That's a dull sort of answer, and I know where that expression came from: "I fear no colours".' (*It seems a poor joke to Maria, who shows herself at least Feste's equal in her combination of scolding and jesting.*)

12-13   **that . . . foolery:** 'you are asking for trouble if you try to jest your way out' (*Maria knows Olivia is in no mood for jesting.*)

14-15   *Feste is saying that a Fool has only one gift, his foolery, so he has to make use of it to excuse himself.*

19-20   *Feste refuses to be put off by Maria's threats; if he is hanged, he may have saved himself from the worse fate of marrying a nagging woman; if he is dismissed he will not manage so badly, as it is now summer, when he will not suffer so much from being unemployed.*

20   **bear it out:** make things easier for me

22   *Maria takes 'points' to mean the metal ends to the strings which held up the Elizabethan breeches—'gaskins', hence her joke which Feste is ready to applaud.*

25-27   'If only Sir Toby were sober enough to realise it, he'd be hard put to it to find a cleverer wife than you.' (*This is the first of several hints to the audience of the possibility of such a marriage.*)

29   **you were best:** that's your best course

30   *Feste is both worried about his imminent telling-off, and yet confident that he can joke his way out of this scrape; so he half seriously invokes the help of the god of wit to inspire him.*

31   **wits:** so-called wise men (*One of Feste's chief functions in the play is going to be to question the wisdom of those who suppose they are wise. His first 'victim' is Olivia.*)

33   **Quinapalus:** *Feste believes that if you don't know a quotation, then you should make one up; and why not make up the name of some learned author who said it also?*

32

| | |
|---|---|
| Maria | Make that good. |
| Feste | He shall see none to fear. |
| Maria | A good lenten answer. I can tell thee where that saying was born, of 'I fear no colours'. |
| Feste | Where, good Mistress Mary? |
| Maria | In the wars; and that may you be bold to say in your foolery. |
| Feste | Well, God give them wisdom that have it; and those that are fools, let them use their talents. |
| Maria | Yet you will be hanged for being so long absent; or, to be turned away, is not that as good as a hanging to you? |
| Feste | Many a good hanging prevents a bad marriage; and, for turning away, let summer bear it out. |
| Maria | You are resolute, then? |
| Feste | Not so neither; but I am resolved on two points. |
| Maria | That if one break, the other will hold; or, if both break, your gaskins fall. |
| Feste | Apt in good faith, very apt. Well, go thy way. If Sir Toby would leave drinking, thou wert as witty a piece of Eve's flesh as any in Illyria. |
| Maria | Peace, you rogue, no more of that; here comes my lady. Make your excuse wisely, you were best. |

*Exit*

| | |
|---|---|
| Feste | Wit, an it be thy will, put me into good fooling! Those wits that think they have thee do very oft prove fools; and I, that am sure I lack thee, may pass for a wise man. For what says Quinapalus? 'Better a witty fool than a foolish wit'. |

*Enter* Olivia, Malvolio *and attendants*

God bless thee, lady.

36     *Olivia's first words are stern and suited to a lady whose sorrow allows her no time for jesting, but Olivia, like so many of the play's characters, is not as she first appears. She will soon be speaking in Feste's defence.*

38–39    'Be off with you—your fooling has become boring; I've had enough of you; besides, I can't trust you any longer.' (*now that he has been absent without leave*)

40–52    *The speed of Feste's thought leaves most minds baffled, and this is probably the intention. Yet his intention is also to convince Olivia that her 'virtue' should pardon his 'sin'. He does this by arguing that as neither virtue nor sin is completely pure, 'unpatched', they have something in common and should tolerate each other.*

40      **madonna:** my lady (*Exaggerated reverence*)

44      **botcher:** a tailor who puts clumsy patches on clothes

47–49    **If that this . . . remedy?:** 'If this straightforward (*said ironically*) form of argument will convince you—all well and good; if not, there's nothing I can do about it.'

49–50    **As there . . . calamity:** 'It's when disaster ("calamity") strikes that a person lets himself be well and truly deceived'

49      **cuckold:** a husband whose wife was unfaithful

50      **so beauty's a flower:** *In the same way, Olivia is deceiving herself if she forgets that beauty is like a flower that quickly fades. The sorrow she feels at her bereavement—the 'calamity'—has deceived her into making the vow, and she is likely to realise too late that in 7 years' time her beauty, and so her chance of marrying, will have vanished.*

54–56    'A complete misunderstanding! Don't judge a man by his appearance (*the Latin literally means: 'a cowl doesn't make a monk'*), in other words, I am not the fool that I seem to be.'

56      **motley:** a jester's long coat was made of motley, a coarse woollen cloth of a variety of colours, but with a dull green predominating

59      **dexteriously:** most skilfully

61      **catechise you:** ask you some questions

62      **mouse of virtue:** *The names Feste uses for Olivia would not seem cheeky coming from the family jester; they continue his argument, for he is still identifying Olivia with what the world calls virtue.*

63–64    'Because I have nothing better to pass the time away with, I'll let you try to prove that.' (*Olivia is clearly bored already by her efforts to remain in seclusion. It is no wonder that curiosity overcomes her resolution, both now and when Cesario appears.*)

| | |
|---|---|
| Olivia | Take the fool away. |
| Feste | Do you not hear, fellows? Take away the lady. |
| Olivia | Go to, you are a dry fool; I'll no more of you; besides, you grow dishonest. |
| Feste | Two faults, madonna, that drink and good 40 counsel will amend; for, give the dry fool drink, then is the fool not dry; bid the dishonest man mend himself—if he mend, he is no longer dishonest; if he cannot, let the botcher mend him. Anything that's mended is but patched; virtue that transgresses is but patched with sin, and sin that amends is but patched with virtue. If that this simple syllogism will serve, so; if it will not, what remedy? As there is no true cuckold but calamity, so beauty's a flower. The lady bade 50 take away the fool; therefore, I say again, take her away. |
| Olivia | Sir, I bade them take away you. |
| Feste | Misprision in the highest degree! Lady, *cucullus non facit monachum*; that's as much to say as I wear not motley in my brain. Good madonna, give me leave to prove you a fool. |
| Olivia | Can you do it? |
| Feste | Dexteriously, good madonna. |
| Olivia | Make your proof. 60 |
| Feste | I must catechise you for it, madonna. Good my mouse of virtue, answer me. |
| Olivia | Well, sir, for want of other idleness I'll bide your proof. |
| Feste | Good madonna, why mournest thou? |
| Olivia | Good fool, for my brother's death. |
| Feste | I think his soul is in hell, madonna. |

72    **Malvolio:** the name of Olivia's steward is meant to soun 
       like the Italian for 'ill-will', malevolence

74    *Malvolio has stood silently in attendance since he came in; now, aske*
       *whether he sees signs of improvement in Feste, he brings to the pla*
       *the first touch of deliberate unpleasantness. He enjoys being able t *
       *rebuke others.*

74–76    'Yes, he's improving all right—the closer he gets to death
       Illness destroys the brain of a wise man, but there's nothin 
       like illness to improve a fool' (*by making him give up jesting*)

77–80    *Malvolio has compared himself, 'a wise man', with the Fool, s *
       *Feste continues the comparison to show how different they are. He ha*
       *none of Malvolio's low-down foxiness, but Malvolio has much o *
       *Feste's supposed folly.*

82–89    'I am surprised that your ladyship gets any pleasure out o 
       such a feeble creature. The other day I saw him outwitted b 
       some amateur fool—one of those you find in low-grad 
       eating-houses and who has about as much intelligence as  
       stone. Just look at him, will you—he's got no defence h 
       can offer; if you didn't laugh at him and thereby give hi 
       the chance to be funny, then he wouldn't be able to say  
       word. I don't mind telling you, I consider that intelligen 
       people, who guffaw at these fools as they artificially try to b 
       funny, are themselves as stupid as the idiots who make fool
       of themselves assisting and imitating professional jesters 
       (*Malvolio in many ways behaves differently from the other characters*
       *Here he declines to argue with Feste or answer his gibe. But he is no*
       *content to be different from the rest; he considers his attitude the onl*
       *right one for anyone with any sense, even going so far as to impl*
       *Olivia is wrong.*)

90–97    'Your trouble, Malvolio, is that you consider nobody perfec 
       except yourself; so you are bitterly critical of everyone els 
       A forgiving, saintly, warm-hearted man would find littl 
       harm in those things that you think are so sinful—it's lik 
       calling cannon-balls the blunt wooden-headed arrows fo 
       knocking down birds. You can't start criticising a jeste 
       because he's abusive—after all, you pay him to be; it ma 
       seem just as like abuse when a man whom everyone knows i 
       dependable spends all his time reprimanding others.' (*Al *
       *though she is defending Feste, Olivia softens her criticism of Malvoli *
       *by flattering him*—'a known discreet man'.)

98–99    'May the god of liars always inspire you with a ready lie 

| | |
|---|---|
| Olivia | I know his soul is in heaven, fool. |
| Feste | The more fool, madonna, to mourn for your brother's soul, being in heaven. Take away the fool, gentlemen. 70 |
| Olivia | What think you of this fool, Malvolio? Doth he not mend? |
| Malv. | Yes, and shall do, till the pangs of death shake him; infirmity, that decays the wise, doth ever make the better fool. |
| Feste | God send you, sir, a speedy infirmity, for the better increasing your folly. Sir Toby will be sworn that I am no fox, but he will not pass his word for two pence that you are no fool. 80 |
| Olivia | How say you to that, Malvolio? |
| Malv. | I marvel your ladyship takes delight in such a barren rascal. I saw him put down the other day with an ordinary fool that has no more brain than a stone. Look you now, he's out of his guard already; unless you laugh and minister occasion to him, he is gagged. I protest, I take these wise men, that crow so at these set kind of fools, no better than the fools' zanies. |
| Olivia | O, you are sick of self-love, Malvolio, and taste 90 with a distempered appetite. To be generous, guiltless, and of free disposition, is to take those things for bird-bolts that you deem cannon-bullets; there is no slander in an allowed fool, though he do nothing but rail; nor no railing in a known discreet man, though he do nothing but reprove. |
| Feste | Now Mercury endue thee with leasing, for thou speakest well of fools! |

104    **well attended:** *Orsino had sent others with Cesario to show that this was a fully authorised visit.*

105    **hold him in delay:** 'are looking after him while he waits'

107–110    'For goodness sake, get someone to remove Sir Toby out of his way—he talks just like a madman, the rogue that he is! Malvolio, will you go, and, if it's someone with a message from the Count, tell him I'm not well or not in; tell him what you like, so long as you get rid of him.'

111–112    *With Malvolio out of hearing, Olivia has just time to show that she is still cross with Feste; he must not think that her recent words mean that she has changed her mind about his fooling.*

113–116    *Feste means that if Sir Toby is an example of Olivia's flesh and blood, any son she may have will need all the brains Jove or Feste can wish for him. The intelligence needed by a professional fool seems all the greater by contrast with Sir Toby who now reels across to Olivia, stammering out his replies.*

116    **pia mater:** brain

121–122    *After his belch, Sir Toby bumps into Feste whom he immediately blames for the collision by calling him a 'sot', a drunken oaf.*

126    *This time Sir Toby is not sober enough to play on words, and genuinely thinks Olivia has accused him of lust rather than of drowsiness.*

*Enter* Maria

Maria    Madam, there is at the gate a young gentleman 100
much desires to speak with you.

Olivia    From the Count Orsino, is it?

Maria    I know not, madam; 'tis a fair young man and
well attended.

Olivia    Who of my people hold him in delay?

Maria    Sir Toby, madam, your kinsman.

Olivia    Fetch him off, I pray you—he speaks nothing but
madman! Fie on him! (*Exit* Maria) Go you, Malvolio; if it be a suit from the count, I am sick or
not at home—what you will, to dismiss it. 110
(*Exit* Malvolio) Now you see, sir, how your
fooling grows old, and people dislike it.

Feste    Thou has spoke for us, madonna, as if thy eldest
son should be a fool; whose skull Jove cram with
brains—for—here he comes—one of thy kin has
a most weak *pia mater*.

*Enter* Sir Toby

Olivia    By mine honour, half drunk! What is he at the
gate, cousin?

Toby    A gentleman.

Olivia    A gentleman! What gentleman?    120

Toby    'Tis a gentleman here—a plague of these pickle-
herring! How now, sot!

Feste    Good Sir Toby—

Olivia    Cousin, cousin, how have you come so early by this
lethargy?

Toby    Lechery! I defy lechery! There's one at the gate.

Olivia    Ay, marry, what is he?

128–129    'He may be the devil for all I care; I've got faith to conquer him, I can tell you.   But what's it all matter?'

131–132    **one . . . heat:** 'one drink more than a man's usual amount' (*which would heat his blood*)

134    **crowner:** coroner (*who would hold an inquest—'sit on'—on a drowned man. Olivia is now quite prepared to join in the joke.*)

137    'He is only at the second stage so far'

    **the fool:** Feste, the professional Fool

139    *Malvolio has carried out Olivia's instructions to the letter, but is baffled by Viola who won't take no for an answer.*

140–142    **he takes . . . with you:** 'he says he knows that already, and has come to speak to you for that very reason' (*Viola is no ordinary messenger; she knows beforehand the sort of excuse a woman will make to avoid receiving an unwelcome visitor.*)

145    **fortified against:** has the answer to

148    *Orsino had told Cesario to be prepared to take root outside the gate, rather than be turned away. Viola is only changing the metaphor.*

149    **a sheriff's post:** a specially impressive post outside the magistrate's

    **supporter:** post supporting

152    'Just an ordinary sort of man' (*Curiosity to see this determined messenger overcomes Olivia's previous resolution to have nothing to do with Orsino. She again has second thoughts.*)

154    *Malvolio is annoyed, not just making puns for fun.*

| Toby | Let him be the devil an he will, I care not; give me faith, say I. Well, it's all one. |
|---|---|

*Exit*

| Olivia | What's a drunken man like, fool? | 130 |
|---|---|---|
| Feste | Like a drowned man, a fool and a madman; one draught above heat makes him a fool, the second mads him, and the third drowns him. | |
| Olivia | Go thou and seek the crowner, and let him sit on my coz, for he's in the third degree of drink; he's drowned. Go, look after him. | |
| Feste | He is but mad yet, madonna, and the fool shall look to the madman. | |

*Exit*

*Enter* Malvolio

| Malv. | Madam, yond young fellow swears he will speak with you. I told him you were sick; he takes on him to understand so much, and therefore comes to speak with you. I told him you were asleep; he seems to have a foreknowledge of that too, and therefore comes to speak with you. What is to be said to him, lady? He's fortified against any denial. | 140 |
|---|---|---|
| Olivia | Tell him he shall not speak with me. | |
| Malv. | Has been told so; and he says he'll stand at your door like a sheriff's post, and be the supporter to a bench, but he'll speak with you. | 150 |
| Olivia | What kind of man is he? | |
| Malv. | Why, of mankind. | |
| Olivia | What manner of man? | |
| Malv. | Of very ill manner; he'll speak with you, will you or no. | |

157–163    *It is an accurate report, though not a very flattering one. As Malvolio says, Cesario is neither one thing nor the other—though only the audience understands why.*

158–163    **as a squash . . . of him:** 'He's like a young pod of peas before the peas are fully ripe, or like a small apple which has still to ripen. The fact is that he's in that in-between stage when the tide is neither ebbing nor flowing—not a boy any longer, but not yet a man. He's very good-looking (*Malvolio is grudgingly honest*) and his voice is just like a woman's. You'd think his mother had just finished weaning him.'

166    *Maria arranges the veil over Olivia's face so that she can keep her promise to hide herself away from the gaze of strangers. This explains why Viola is unsure which is Olivia and why her language remains almost comically formal until she is amazed by Olivia's beauty.*

167    **embassy:** message

170    *Viola begins to declaim Orsino's message which she has learned by heart, 'conned', then breaks off as Maria and the other women in attendance, 'good beauties', laugh at her. She is still not sure which lady to address.*

175–176    **let me . . . usage:** 'do not mock me; I am easily put off by the slightest signs of rudeness'

179–180    **give . . . assurance if:** 'give me some reasonable sign to show that' (*Viola would like to see her rival's face.*)

182    **a comedian:** an actor of some sort (*Viola has started to declaim a speech and is now overplaying her bewilderment. Olivia is losing patience with Orsino's messenger.*)

183    **No, my profound heart:** 'No, my clever young lady' (*Viola means that Olivia is nearer the truth than she realises: Viola is, after all, playing a part.*)

183–184    **by the . . . play:** 'as bad luck will have it, I am not what I appear to be' (*This is said more to the audience than to Olivia to remind them of the difficult part her disguise forces her to play.*)

| | |
|---|---|
| Olivia | Of what personage and years is he? |
| Malv. | Not yet old enough for a man, nor young enough for a boy; as a squash is before 'tis a peascod, or a codling when 'tis almost an apple; 'tis with him in standing water, between boy and 160 man. He is very well-favoured, and he speaks very shrewishly; one would think his mother's milk were scarce out of him. |
| Olivia | Let him approach. Call in my gentlewoman. |
| Malv. | Gentlewoman, my lady calls. |

*Exit*

*Enter* Maria

| | |
|---|---|
| Olivia | Give me my veil; come, throw it o'er my face; We'll once more hear Orsino's embassy. |

*Enter* Viola *and attendants*

| | |
|---|---|
| Viola | The honourable lady of the house, which is she? |
| Olivia | Speak to me; I shall answer for her. Your will? |
| Viola | Most radiant, exquisite and unmatchable beauty! 170 —I pray you tell me if this be the lady of the house, for I never saw her. I would be loth to cast away my speech, for, besides that it is excellently well penned, I have taken great pains to con it. Good beauties, let me sustain no scorn; I am very comptible, even to the least sinister usage. |
| Olivia | Whence came you, sir? |
| Viola | I can say little more than I have studied, and that question's out of my part. Good gentle one, give me modest assurance if you be the lady of the 180 house, that I may proceed in my speech. |
| Olivia | Are you a comedian? |
| Viola | No, my profound heart; and yet—by the very |

186, 187    **usurp:** *Olivia playfully says:* 'If I am play-acting, I am only acting myself.' *Viola takes the word 'usurp' in its full sense of* holding on to something that doesn't belong to you *to accuse Olivia of acting unnaturally if she refuses to give her beauty to a husband and keeps it only for her own enjoyment.*

189    **from my commission:** not what I was told to say

191    **the heart:** the important part

192    **I forgive you:** I'll let you off (*We are spared Orsino's poetry because Olivia is anxious to hear Cesario speak for himself and about himself.*)

196–202    'Then it's all the more likely to be fictitious; so please forget it. I heard of your cheekiness while you were waiting outside, and I had you brought here, not to hear what you had to say, but to satisfy my curiosity. You had better be off now unless you are a complete idiot. If you are sensible, you'll clear off quickly. I'm not in the mood now for joining in such a trivial kind of conversation.' (*Olivia suggests Cesario may have caught some of his master's disease, the lover's madness which was likely to become more frenzied at a full moon.*)

203    *Maria thinks that Olivia has given her the cue to get rid of the tiresome messenger. Viola, however, is quite able to cope with Maria, metaphors and all, even though she pretends to ask Olivia's help to restrain such a 'giant'—Maria is rather small!*

204–206    'No, my fine deck-washer, I shall be drifting here a little longer. Do please restrain your giant with something, dear lady.'

209–211    'You must have something frightfully serious to say, when you are such a long time in getting to the point. Well, say what you have come to say.'

212–215    *Viola says that Olivia need not fear to be alone with her, nor is her message earth-shattering.*

212    **overture:** declaration

213    **taxation of:** demands for

     **olive:** *The olive branch symbolised peace.*

| | |
|---|---|
| | fangs of malice, I swear—I am not that I play. Are you the lady of the house? |
| Olivia | If I do not usurp myself, I am. |
| Viola | Most certain, if you are she, you do usurp yourself; for what is yours to bestow is not yours to reserve. But this is from my commission. I will on with my speech in your praise, and then show 190 you the heart of my message. |
| Olivia | Come to what is important in it; I forgive you the praise. |
| Viola | Alas, I took great pains to study it, and 'tis poetical. |
| Olivia | It is the more like to be feigned; I pray you, keep it in. I heard you were saucy at my gates, and allowed your approach rather to wonder at you than to hear you. If you be not mad, be gone; if you have reason, be brief; 'tis not that time of 200 moon with me to make one in so skipping a dialogue. |
| Maria | Will you hoist sail, sir? Here lies your way. |
| Viola | No, good swabber, I am to hull here a little longer. Some mollification for your giant, sweet lady. |
| Olivia | Tell me your mind. |
| Viola | I am a messenger. |
| Olivia | Sure, you have some hideous matter to deliver, when the courtesy of it is so fearful. Speak your 210 office. |
| Viola | It alone concerns your ear. I bring no overture of war, no taxation of homage; I hold the olive in my hand; my words are as full of peace as matter. |

218–221    'What you call my rudeness was copied from the way I have been treated since I came here. Who I am and what I have to say are so sacred that only you must hear it; it would be a disgrace if anyone else heard it.' (*Safe in her disguise, Viola can so nearly speak the truth: her identity is as secret as (her) virginity,* 'maidenhead'.)

222    **Give us the place alone:** 'Let us have the place to ourselves' (*Playfully Olivia interrogates Cesario by continuing the metaphor— love is a kind of religion. The meaning of what they are saying is to both of them less important than keeping going this rally of words:* 'divinity', 'profanation', 'text', 'doctrine', 'chapter', 'heresy'.)

224    'What is it that you came to say?'

226–227    'That's a comforting thing to believe (that I'm a sweet lady) and a lot can be said on the subject, but where does it come from?'

230    **by the method:** 'if I have to continue this metaphorical way of talking'

    **the first:** the opening chapter and so the most important

231    **it is heresy:** 'I should be a fool to believe it'

236    *Olivia makes only the mildest protest before she breaks her vow and very readily shows Cesario her beauty,* 'the picture', *by drawing back her veil,* 'the curtain'.

237–238    **such . . . done:** 'this is what I used to look like (before I took to wearing a veil); a fine piece of work, isn't it?'

239    *Rather rudely Viola queries how much of Olivia's beauty is due to make-up. Her woman's curiosity about her rival is too strong for Viola to restrain. Ladies were often criticised for painting their faces to disguise blemishes etc., and Olivia has given Viola the opening by talking of her face as a portrait.*

240    **in grain:** permanent, and therefore natural

241    *Viola quite spontaneously comes out with a gasp of admiration, which she quickly turns to a criticism of Olivia's selfishness in keeping the enjoyment of her beauty to herself. As the conversation becomes more serious and emotional, the prose slips into verse, despite Olivia's attempt to brush off the flattery by replying at first in prose.*

241–245    'It is beauty so perfectly blending the white and the red that you'd think nature herself had been the artist whose skill had fashioned such a complexion. Oh, you are the cruellest lady in the world if you mean to let this beauty die with you, without leaving behind you a copy!' (*that is, a child who would inherit Olivia's beauty*)

| | |
|---|---|
| Olivia | Yet you began rudely. What are you? What would you? |
| Viola | The rudeness that hath appeared in me have I learned from my entertainment. What I am, and what I would, are as secret as maidenhead—to 220 your ears, divinity; to any other's, profanation. |
| Olivia | Give us the place alone; we will hear this divinity. |

*Exit* Maria *and attendants*

| | |
|---|---|
| | Now, sir, what is your text? |
| Viola | Most sweet lady— |
| Olivia | A comfortable doctrine, and much may be said of it. Where lies your text? |
| Viola | In Orsino's bosom. |
| Olivia | In his bosom! In what chapter of his bosom? |
| Viola | To answer by the method, in the first of his heart. 230 |
| Olivia | O, I have read it; it is heresy. Have you no more to say? |
| Viola | Good madam, let me see your face. |
| Olivia | Have you any commission from your lord to negotiate with my face? You are now out of your text. But we will draw the curtain and show you the picture. Look you, sir, such a one I was as this present; is it not well done? |
| Viola | Excellently done—if God did all. |
| Olivia | 'Tis in grain, sir; 'twill endure wind and weather. 240 |
| Viola | 'Tis beauty truly blent, whose red and white Nature's own sweet and cunning hand laid on: Lady, you are the cruellest she alive, If you will lead these graces to the grave, And leave the world no copy. |

| | |
|---|---|
| 246 | *Half-playfully, half-scornfully, Olivia suggests another way for her beauty to become immortal.* |
| 246–250 | **I will give . . . red**: 'I will distribute a number of detailed descriptions of my beauty. I'll have a list drawn up and every part and parcel of my beauty I'll have added to my will; for example: lot number one—two lips of a reasonable shade of red' |
| 253 | *Scorn is met by scorn. Olivia speaks harshly because she has no feeling for Orsino; Viola, because she so admires him.* |
| 255–257 | 'If you were the most beautiful woman in the world, and you were to marry him, then it would be no more than the due reward for such love as his.' |
| 258 | **nonpareil**: a person who is unequalled anywhere |
| 260 | **fertile tears**: floods of tears (*There is nothing comical to Viola about Orsino's passionate way of loving. This is a list of an Elizabethan courtier's ways of showing his love, yet, no doubt, a man who imagined himself in love could easily summon up tears and moans.*) |
| 263–268 | *This is a timely reminder of Orsino's good qualities. He is really a fine man, fit for Viola to fall in love with. Olivia makes it quite clear that she has her eyes wide open, and that there is no possibility of her marrying Orsino.* |
| 263 | **Yet I suppose him**: I am sure he is |
| 264 | **Of . . . youth**: 'an active young man who has done no wrong to anybody' |
| 265 | **In voices well divulged**: Well spoken of by people in general |
| | **free**: generous |
| 267 | 'in physique and appearance' |
| 270–273 | 'If I loved you with the same passion as my master feels; if I were suffering as he is; and if I were half-dead from rejected love; then I wouldn't believe it possible for you to refuse me; I would be incapable of accepting it.' |
| 274 | *Olivia is deliberately prompting Cesario to show how he can speak of love.* |
| 275 | **willow**: the tree associated with weeping lovers |
| 275–283 | '(If I were Orsino, I would) build myself a shelter of willow branches outside your house, and cry aloud to my loved one, my better self, within the house. I would write verse dedicated to my rejected love, and sing it for all the world to hear at the dead of night. I would shout your name to the echoing |

| | |
|---|---|
| Olivia | O, sir, I will not be so hard-hearted; I will give out divers schedules of my beauty. It shall be inventoried, and every particle and utensil labelled to my will; as: item—two lips indifferent red; item—two grey eyes with lids to them; 250 item—one neck, one chin, and so forth. Were you sent hither to praise me? |
| Viola | I see you what you are; you are too proud. But, if you were the devil, you are fair. My lord and master loves you. O, such love Could be but recompensed, though you were crowned The nonpareil of beauty! |
| Olivia | How does he love me? |
| Viola | With adorations, fertile tears,     260 With groans that thunder love, with sighs of fire. |
| Olivia | Your lord does know my mind; I cannot love him. Yet I suppose him virtuous, know him noble, Of great estate, of fresh and stainless youth, In voices well divulged, free, learned and valiant, And in dimension and the shape of nature A gracious person; but yet I cannot love him. He might have took his answer long ago. |
| Viola | If I did love you in my master's flame,     270 With such a suffering, such a deadly life, In your denial I would find no sense; I would not understand it. |
| Olivia | Why, what would you? |
| Viola | Make me a willow cabin at your gate, And call upon my soul within the house; Write loyal cantons of contemned love, And sing them loud even in the dead of night; |

hills and make the echo, that chatterbox of the air, cry out after me 'Olivia'. There would be no peace for you from these voices calling my love to you from the hills and air, until you took pity on me.' (*This is not just an eloquent piece of romantic poetry; it is dramatically appropriate. Viola's frustrated love at last has a chance to express itself. This is the way Viola longs to cry to the world, not Olivia's, but Orsino's name.*)

279   **Holla:** *The echo would pick up the word* 'Holla' *and make it sound like* 'Olivia'.

284   *Not surprisingly, Olivia's curiosity is aroused by this passionate outburst, and further provoked by Cesario's riddle of an answer.*

286–287   'Better than my present condition suggests, although my true social position is a high one. I come from a noble family.'

290–291   *A thin excuse leaving the way open for a possible return by Cesario.*

292   **this:** the purse which Cesario rejects

293   **fee'd post:** messenger who needs paying

295   *Viola's prayer that Olivia should suffer comes swiftly true. Ironically, Viola is to be the* 'heart of flint'.

296–297   'May the god of love harden the heart of whatever man you fall in love with, so that your consuming love, like my master's, is treated with contempt.'

303   **give . . . blazon** 'are five strong proofs that you are a gentleman'
        **blazon:** a heraldic coat of arms

304–305   **soft! . . . man:** 'but just wait a minute! Suppose the servant should turn out to be the lord!'

306   *Olivia is about to be as infatuated as Orsino thinks he is, but, unlike him, she always has the ability to see herself as others see her, and so shares in the ridiculousness of her situation.*
        **plague:** love

309   *Olivia is not prepared to fight against love, and immediately takes action to help promote it.*

|           | Holla your name to the reverberate hills, |      |
|-----------|--------------------------------------------|------|
|           | And make the babbling gossip of the air    | 280  |
|           | Cry out 'Olivia!' O, you should not rest    |      |
|           | Between the elements of air and earth,      |      |
|           | But you should pity me.                     |      |

Olivia   You might do much.
    What is your parentage?

Viola   Above my fortunes, yet my state is well;
    I am a gentleman.

Olivia   Get you to your lord.
    I cannot love him; let him send no more.
    Unless, perchance, you come to me again,          290
    To tell me how he takes it. Fare you well.
    I thank you for your pains; spend this for me.

Viola   I am no fee'd post, lady; keep your purse.
    My master, not myself, lacks recompense.
    Love make his heart of flint that you shall love,
    And let your fervour, like my master's, be
    Placed in contempt. Farewell, fair cruelty.

*Exit*

Olivia   'What is your parentage?'
    'Above my fortunes, yet my state is well;
    I am a gentleman.' I'll be sworn thou art!          300
    Thy tongue, thy face, thy limbs, actions and
    spirit,
        Do give thee five-fold blazon.
    Not too fast! Soft, soft!
    Unless the master were the man. How now!
    Even so quickly may one catch the plague?
    Methinks I feel this youth's perfections,
    With an invisible and subtle stealth,
    To creep in at mine eyes. Well, let it be.

312 **peevish:** tiresome

314 **Would I:** Whether I wanted it

315 **flatter with:** encourage, *by giving Orsino a false account of how Olivia feels*

317–318 *A hint, which would not escape any intelligent messenger, that Olivia would welcome his return.*

318 **Hie thee:** Hurry up (*Olivia almost pushes Malvolio after Cesario.*)

320–323 'What can I be thinking of to do that? I'm afraid I shall find love is making a fool of me. All right, Fate, let's see what you can do! We can't be held responsible for what we do.'

322 **owe:** own

323 *This is not accepting one's fate like some tragic heroine, but slyly shifting the responsibility to Fate, while adding a footnote that she will be quite happy provided that things turn out as she wants them!*

What ho, Malvolio!

*Enter* Malvolio

| | |
|---|---|
| Malv. | Here, madam, at your service. |
| Olivia | Run after that same peevish messenger, |

The count's man; he left this ring behind him,
Would I or not. Tell him I'll none of it.
Desire him not to flatter with his lord,
Nor hold him up with hopes; I am not for him.
If that the youth will come this way tomorrow,
I'll give him reasons for it. Hie thee, Malvolio.

Malv.　　Madam, I will.

*Exit*

Olivia　　I do I know not what, and fear to find　　320
Mine eye too great a flatterer for my mind.
Fate, show thy force; ourselves we do not owe;
What is decreed must be—and be this so!

*Exit*

Sebastian's arrival from the shipwreck has been expected since Viola's optimism in the second scene. This brief conversation reassures the audience that both Sebastian and Antonio are likely at any time to enter Viola's new surroundings. As Sebastian is dressed like Viola, more confusion can be expected when he arrives at court.

1–2   **will you not that I**: won't you let me

3   **By your patience, no**: 'If you don't mind, I'd rather you didn't.' (*Sebastian's language is more difficult to understand than Viola's; he lacks both her way of saying exactly what she means and her touches of imagination.*)

3–4   *Unlike Viola, Sebastian blames the stars for his misfortune,* 'malignancy', *and discourages Antonio from accompanying him lest he is affected also by this misfortune.*

5   **distemper**: ruin

5–6   **Therefore . . . leave**: *A polite way of asking to be left alone.*

10–14   'To be honest with you, all I intend doing is having a look around. I note with approval your restraint, which is such that you are not likely to press me to tell you what I prefer to keep secret; however, I think I owe it to you to tell you about myself. The facts are these, then:' (*Antonio knows his place and so would not presume to question Sebastian as to who he is—he is obviously a gentleman and Antonio an ordinary captain. Sebastian, however, thinks he owes it to his rescuer to tell him who he has rescued.*)

16   **Roderigo**: *Sebastian, in a foreign country, had also taken a false name, which, in fact, he doesn't have occasion to use. It is one complication that can fortunately be forgotten.*

18   **left behind**: *when he died*

20   **so ended**: 'died together, as we were born together—in the same hour'

22   **breach**: breaking waves

25–32   'She was a lady who, despite looking like me, was generally considered beautiful. Though, in all modesty, I couldn't agree with such a flattering comment, yet I will go so far as

# ACT 2

SCENE 1    Another part of Illyria
*Enter* Antonio *and* Sebastian.

Antonio    Will you stay no longer? Nor will you not that
           I go with you?

Sebas.     By your patience, no. My stars shine darkly over
           me; the malignancy of my fate might perhaps
           distemper yours. Therefore I shall crave of you
           your leave that I may bear my evils alone. It
           were a bad recompense for your love to lay any
           of them on you.

Antonio    Let me yet know of you whither you are bound.

Sebas.     No, sooth, sir; my determinate voyage is mere    10
           extravagancy. But I perceive in you so excellent
           a touch of modesty, that you will not extort from
           me what I am willing to keep in; therefore it
           charges me in manners the rather to express
           myself. You must know of me then, Antonio,
           my name is Sebastian, which I called Roderigo.
           My father was that Sebastian of Messaline, whom
           I know you have heard of. He left behind him
           myself and a sister, both born in an hour; if the
           heavens had been pleased, would we had so ended!   20
           But you, sir, altered that; for, some hour before
           you took me from the breach of the sea, was my
           sister drowned.

Antonio    Alas the day!

Sebas.     A lady, sir, though it was said she much re-
           sembled me, was yet of many accounted beauti-
           ful; but though I could not with such estimable

to say this about her, that not even a jealous woman rival would have denied her nobility. And now she is drowned in the sea and all I can do is shed tears (more salt water) when I remember her.' (*Sebastian is very eager not to be seen as praising himself when he speaks of Viola's beauty.*)

33    *Sadness gets the better of him and he cannot stop himself from weeping. Antonio, now knowing what Sebastian has gone through, apologises for having looked after him so inadequately.*

34    **your trouble:** 'the trouble you have gone to on my behalf'

37–38    *Affection and exaggeration are catching. Sebastian means that Antonio is overwhelmingly generous.*

39    **kindness:** *Sebastian feels he would not be normal, a member of mankind, if he didn't feel like crying. His sorrow has built up inside him and is forcing its way out.*

40    **manners of my mother:** *crying was thought unmanly*

42    **tell tales:** weep, and so betray his unmanly feelings

45    *It is curious at first to think of danger being associated with Orsino's court, but this reminds us that Illyria is a foreign country to Sebastian and Antonio.*

47–48    *Antonio stands alone for a minute uncertain whether to follow Sebastian or to think of his own safety. Then friendship gets the better of him and he hastens after Sebastian.*

### Scene 2

The previous scene has occupied the few minutes it would take Malvolio to overtake Cesario. When he has gone, Viola has one of her rare moments alone on the stage, a chance to show how she is patiently resigned to the difficulties of her situation. Her speech is a help to any of the audience who may still be muddled by the very complicated story.

1    *Malvolio is annoyed that he is being used as a messenger and so, as soon as he catches up with Cesario, he does not greet him politely, but questions him sharply.*
       **even:** just

2–3    'I was there, sir, just a minute or two ago, and I have reached as far as this at a moderate walking pace.' (*Viola restrains herself and gives a coldly factual reply.*)

wonder over-far believe that, yet thus far I will boldly publish her: she bore a mind that envy could not but call fair. She is drowned already, sir, with salt water, though I seem to drown her remembrance again with more.

30

Antonio      Pardon me, sir, your bad entertainment.

Sebas.      O, good Antonio, forgive me your trouble.

Antonio      If you will not murder me for my love, let me be your servant.

Sebas.      If you will not undo what you have done—that is, kill him whom you have recovered—desire it not. Fare ye well at once. My bosom is full of kindness, and I am yet so near the manners of my mother, that, upon the least occasion more, mine eyes will tell tales of me. I am bound to the Count Orsino's court; farewell.

40

*Exit*

Antonio      The gentleness of all the gods go with thee!
I have many enemies in Orsino's court,
Else would I very shortly see thee there.
    But, come what may, I do adore thee so
That danger shall seem sport, and I will go.

*Exit*


SCENE 2    A street in Illyria
*Enter* Viola *followed by* Malvolio.


Malv.      Were not you even now with the Countess Olivia?

Viola      Even now, sir; on a moderate pace, I have since arrived but hither.

4   *Malvolio is good at his job as Olivia's steward, and he accurately delivers her message, but he first takes the chance to show his annoyance.*

7   **put . . . assurance:** 'convince him that there is no hope for him'

9   **hardy:** rash

12   **I'll none of it:** 'I don't want it' (*Understanding that the ring is a love-token from Olivia, Viola quickly invents a lie about the ring to stop Malvolio guessing the truth about Olivia.*)

13–16   *Malvolio does little more than repeat what Olivia told him, even using the same description—'peevishly'; then he scornfully throws what he thinks is Cesario's ring on to the ground. He is not going to waste more words with a servant.*

15   **in your eye:** where you can see it

17   *Viola speaks her thoughts aloud, giving the audience plenty of chance to see that she is honestly upset by the trouble her disguise is causing other people. She is the only one of the trio—Orsino, Olivia and Viola—who is unselfish enough to pity someone else. This is all the more surprising when that someone else is her rival, Olivia.*

18–24   'I hope to goodness she hasn't been attracted by my appearance. She had a good look at me; in fact, I thought at times she had swallowed her tongue—she was so busy watching me, only half aware of what she was saying. It must be that she is in love with me, and has found this subtle way of letting me know of her love, by using this rude messenger (Malvolio).'

28–33   'What a deceitful thing a disguise is; it is so easy for the resourceful devil (the 'enemy' of mankind) to use it for his evil purposes. Women's hearts are like wax; it is all too easy for a man to pretend to be an attractive lover and make a deep impression there. It's women's weak nature that's to blame; you can't blame us; if we're made that way, it's not our fault.' (*Viola is quite prepared to admit that she shares Olivia's fault; after all, it did not take long for her to become infatuated by Orsino.*)

30   **proper-false:** men who are attractive yet deceivers

34–41   'How is this going to turn out? My master is head over heels in love with her; I—odd creature that I am—dote just as

| Malv. | She returns this ring to you, sir. You might have saved me my pains, to have taken it away yourself. She adds, moreover, that you should put your lord into a desperate assurance she will none of him. And one thing more: that you be never so hardy to come again in his affairs, unless it be to report your lord's taking of this. Receive it so. | 10 |

| Viola | She took the ring of me; I'll none of it. | |

| Malv. | Come, sir, you peevishly threw it to her; and her will is it should be so returned. If it be worth stooping for, there it lies in your eye; if not, be it his that finds it. | |

*Exit*

| Viola | I left no ring with her; what means this lady? | |
| | Fortune forbid my outside have not charmed her. | |
| | She made good view of me; indeed so much | |
| | That sure methought her eyes had lost her tongue, | 20 |
| | For she did speak in starts distractedly. | |
| | She loves me, sure; the cunning of her passion | |
| | Invites me in this churlish messenger. | |
| | None of my lord's ring! Why, he sent her none! | |
| | I am the man; if it be so, as 'tis, | |
| | Poor lady, she were better love a dream! | |
| | Disguise, I see thou art a wickedness, | |
| | Wherein the pregnant enemy does much. | |
| | How easy is it for the proper-false | 30 |
| | In women's waxen hearts to set their forms! | |
| | Alas, our frailty is the cause, not we, | |
| | For such as we are made of, such we be. | |
| | How will this fadge? My master loves her dearly, | |

much on him; and she is so hoodwinked that she is infatuated by me. What's going to come of all this? Because of my man's disguise, I can have no hope of making Orsino love me. Because I am really a woman—what a mess it all is!—Olivia is going to suffer the agonies of love all for nothing.'

36   **monster:** *Viola thinks her disguise makes her some unnatural thing, neither a man nor a woman.*

## Scene 3

A wildly gay drinking session in the middle of the night is just the thing to provoke Malvolio. His angry interference and his scorn for such low behaviour inspire Sir Toby, under Maria's direction, to lay a trap for their enemy.

1   *Sir Toby beckons to Sir Andrew to share with him this great piece of reasoning: that going to bed in the early hours is highly virtuous! It is a way of letting the audience know that this scene is late at night. The Elizabethans could not darken the stage during their performances. which usually took place in the afternoon.*

2   **betimes:** early

    **diluculo surgere:** the beginning of a well-known proverb—'It's good for your health to get up early'

4–5   *Any sort of a puzzle is too much for Sir Andrew, even when he is not half-drunk.*

6   **as an unfilled can:** *an appropriate comparison to come from Sir Toby who drinks almost non-stop*

10   **four elements:** *The old belief was that everything was made up of varying amounts of earth, air, fire and water. Like many men who are half-drunk, Sir Toby starts to put forward some profound views about life in general. Sir Andrew can only think about his own life.*

13   **Thou art a scholar!:** 'How right you are!' (*said with friendly sarcasm*)

14   **stoup:** jug (*Sir Toby yells off-stage to Maria who must be somewhere in the wine-cellar.*)

16–17   *Feste rudely compares the two knights to the faces of two drunken idiots on an inn sign. Under the sign it would say, 'We three. . . .', meaning the person looking up at it was the third.*

And I, poor monster, fond as much on him;
And she, mistaken, seems to dote on me.
What will become of this? As I am man,
My state is desperate for my master's love;
As I am woman—now, alas the day!—                    40
What thriftless sighs shall poor Olivia breathe!
O time, thou must untangle this, not I;
It is too hard a knot for me to untie.

*Exit*


SCENE 3   Olivia's house
*Enter* Sir Toby *and* Sir Andrew.

Toby      Approach, Sir Andrew. Not to be abed after
          midnight is to be up betimes, and *diluculo surgere*,
          thou knowest—

Andrew    Nay, by my troth, I know not; but I know to be
          up late is to be up late.

Toby      A false conclusion; I hate it as an unfilled can.
          To be up after midnight, and to go to bed then,
          is early; so that to go to bed after midnight is to
          go to bed betimes. Does not our life consist of the
          four elements?                                          10

Andrew    Faith, so they say—but I think it rather consists
          of eating and drinking.

Toby      Thou art a scholar! Let us therefore eat and drink.
          Marian, I say, a stoup of wine!

          *Enter* Feste

Andrew    Here comes the fool, in faith.

Feste     How now, my hearts! Did you never see the pic-
          ture of 'We three'?

18     **catch:** a round, like 'London's burning!', where each singer gave the one before a start, and then tried to 'catch' him up

19     **breast:** singing voice

21     **breath:** voice (*Sir Andrew is most envious of Feste because he can sing, dance, joke and make up the most marvellous nonsense.*)

23–24     **Pigrogromitus, the Vapians, Queubus:** *These words, made up by Feste, seem to have amused Sir Andrew because they sound like comical versions of learned old Roman writers. He was so delighted that he paid Feste for making him laugh—though not over-generously.*

26     **leman:** lady-love

27–29     *Feste is quite happy to go on talking nonsense if he is paid for it, so he continues to make up words, like* 'impeticos' (*for* 'stow it away in my gown') *and* 'gratillity' (*'a small tip', 'gratuity'*). *He explains in his nonsensical way why he has not yet spent Sir Andrew's tip on his girl friend. He gives three reasons, at which a modern audience can only guess: perhaps that he has to be very careful what he does under Malvolio's nose; that the young lady is no common girl to be palmed off with cheap gifts; and that he wasn't able to get hold of any cheap beer to buy it with.*

28     **whipstock:** the handle of a whip

29     **Myrmidons:** the followers of Achilles in the Trojan War (*more of Feste's mockery of learning*)

        **bottle-ale houses:** taverns selling poor-quality ale

34     **testril:** sixpence (*Sir Andrew does not want to be thought mean.*)

        **if one knight give a:** *The first of several occasions in this scene where Sir Andrew has no better model of a knight to copy than Sir Toby. Gradually he seems more and more pathetic as he apes such a preposterous version of knightly conduct.*

35–36, 38     **good life:** food and drink (*but Sir Andrew misunderstands, thinking that Feste is offering to sing about virtue, living the 'good life'*)

39     *The two knights have not yet reached the state of drunken rowdiness. They can sit back and listen dreamily to Feste's simple song as he accompanies himself on his lute. The song's advice to young lovers, not to delay sharing their love, is the same as Feste gave Olivia in 1.v.*

47     'Love isn't something you acquire as you grow older—it's here and now.'

48     'You laugh at a joke as soon as you see its point—it's automatic.'

| | |
|---|---|
| Toby | Welcome, ass. Now, let's have a catch. |
| Andrew | By my troth, the fool has an excellent breast. I had rather than forty shillings I had such a leg, and so sweet a breath to sing, as the fool has. In sooth, thou wast in very gracious fooling last night, when thou spokest of Pigrogromitus, of the Vapians passing the Equinoctial of Queubus; 'twas very good, in faith. I sent thee sixpence for thy leman; hadst it? |
| Feste | I did impeticos thy gratillity; for Malvolio's nose is no whipstock; my lady has a white hand; and the Myrmidons are no bottle-ale houses. |
| Andrew | Excellent! Why, this is the best fooling, when all is done. Now, a song. |
| Toby | Come on, there is sixpence for you. Let's have a song. |
| Andrew | There's a testril of me, too; if one knight give a— |
| Feste | Would you have a love-song, or a song of good life? |
| Toby | A love-song, a love-song. |
| Andrew | Ay, ay, I care not for good life. |
| Feste | (*sings*) O mistress mine, where are you roaming? O stay and hear; your true love's coming, That can sing both high and low. Trip no further, pretty sweeting; Journeys end in lovers meeting, Every wise man's son doth know. |
| Andrew | Excellent good, in faith. |
| Toby | Good, good. |
| Feste | (*sings*) What is love? 'Tis not hereafter; Present mirth hath present laughter; What's to come is still unsure. |

50    'It's no good storing up love, hoping it will grow bigger if
      not used'

51    **sweet-and-twenty:** with twenty sweet kisses

53    **mellifluous:** most sweet

54    **contagious:** evil-smelling (*The word deceives Sir Andrew; he
      thinks Sir Toby is also praising Feste's singing.*)

56    'If you listened with your nose, you could say his voice was
      both sweet and smelly.'

57    **welkin:** sky

58–59  **a catch . . . weaver:** 'a song to make even a weaver's heart
      leap for joy' (*Weavers, who were usually Puritans, were well-known
      for their singing—though their psalm-singing would be rather different
      from this song!*)

59    **three souls:** *According to an old belief, a man had three kinds of
      soul.*

60    'Yes, let's; I'm a great one for those songs.'

61    **catch:** catch rats (*a pun which Sir Andrew again fails to see*)

62–68  *The songs's title is 'Thou knave' and its first line 'Hold thy peace,
      thou knave'. This gives Feste the chance for some obvious jesting
      at Sir Andrew's expense.*

63–64  **I shall . . . knight:** 'If I sing that, then I shall be forced to
      call you a knave, Sir Andrew.' (*Sir Andrew is quite used to being
      so called.*)

69    *Feste eventually begins to sing the first line, then Sir Toby repeats the
      first line, and then Sir Andrew, so that when they are all yelling
      different words, there is such a din that it is not surprising it wakes
      all the household. Maria rushes in to try to give them a friendly
      warning before Malvolio comes in.*

70    **caterwauling:** a frightful noise, like cats in the middle of
      the night (*Sir Toby is too drunk to worry about Maria's warning.
      His mind is so full of bits of popular songs that he keeps breaking
      out into song.*)

73    **Cataian:** Chinese (*an insult which amounted to calling someone
      a cheat*)

      **politicians:** schemers, about some important business

74    **a Peg-a-Ramsey:** the title of a song about a foolish old lover

74–75  **'Three merry men be we':** another song title

75    **consanguineous:** a close relation (*Sir Toby can often surprise
      his friends with a show of learning; unlike Sir Andrew, he has some
      knowledge of the word's meaning too.*)

78    'My word, Sir Toby's on form tonight!'

> In delay there lies no plenty;
> Then come kiss me, sweet-and-twenty;
> Youth's a stuff will not endure.

Andrew    A mellifluous voice, as I am true knight.

Toby    A contagious breath.

Andrew    Very sweet and contagious, in faith.

Toby    To hear by the nose, it is dulcet in contagion. But shall we make the welkin dance indeed? Shall we rouse the night-owl in a catch that will draw three souls out of one weaver? Shall we do that?

Andrew    An you love me, let's do it! I am dog at a catch.    60

Feste    By our lady, sir, and some dogs will catch well.

Andrew    Most certain. Let our catch be 'Thou knave'.

Feste    'Hold thy peace, thou knave', knight. I shall be constrained in it to call thee knave, knight.

Andrew    'Tis not the first time I have constrained one to call me knave. Begin, fool; it begins, 'Hold thy peace'.

Feste    I shall never begin if I hold my peace.

Andrew    Good, in faith. Come, begin.   (*They sing the catch*)

*Enter* Maria

Maria    What a caterwauling do you keep here! If my    70 lady have not called up her steward, Malvolio, and bid him turn you out of doors, never trust me.

Toby    My lady's a Cataian; we are politicians; Malvolio's a Peg-a-Ramsey, and (*sings*) 'Three merry men be we'. Am not I consanguineous? Am I not of her blood? Tillyvally, lady! (*sings*) 'There dwelt a man in Babylon, lady, lady.'

Feste    Beshrew me, the knight's in admirable fooling.

79–81    *As in line 34 Sir Andrew doesn't like to be outdone by Sir Toby. He has to agree that Sir Toby plays the fool very well, but, without realising what he is saying, he insists that he himself is a born fool.*

84    *Malvolio's angry interruption—he is dressed in a long nightgown and carries a candle—only adds to the fun. The three are too drunk to notice his threats, and dance round him insulting him by singing bits of songs about him.*

84–90    'Gentlemen, have you taken leave of your senses? What's come over you? Where's your commonsense, your manners, your sense of decency, that you are bawling away like uncivilised tinkers in the middle of the night? You'd think my lady's house was a tavern the way you are going on, squawking out your drunken songs like common cobblers, without any attempt to moderate and keep your voices down! Don't you have any respect for where you are, for whom you are disturbing, for what time it is?'

91    'You're wrong there—we did keep time; we were all together in our singing. Go away and hang yourself!' (*Sir Toby is delighted to be able to contradict, even if it means punning on* 'time'.)

92–98    'Sir Toby, I see I must speak plainly to you. My lady told me to let you know that, though she lets you stay here because you are her uncle, she will have nothing to do with such disgraceful behaviour. If you can pull yourself together, and stop behaving so irresponsibly, then you are welcome to stay at her house; if not, if you'd be so good as to pack yourself off, she will be only too pleased to see the last of you.' (*Malvolio is only delivering Olivia's message, but his superior way of doing so is what infuriates the revellers. They continue to sing their comments about him like bits of an opera.*)

106    *Sarcastic.*

| | |
|---|---|
| Andrew | Ay, he does well enough if he be disposed, and so do I too. He does it with a better grace, but I do it more natural. 80 |
| Toby | (*sings*) 'O, the twelfth day of December—' |
| Maria | For the love of God, peace! |

*Enter* Malvolio

| | |
|---|---|
| Malv. | My masters, are you mad? Or what are you? Have you no wit, manners nor honesty, but to gabble like tinkers at this time of night? Do ye make an alehouse of my lady's house that ye squeak out your coziers' catches without any mitigation or remorse of voice? Is there no respect of place, persons nor time in you? 90 |
| Toby | We did keep time, sir, in our catches. Sneck up! |
| Malv. | Sir Toby, I must be round with you. My lady bade me tell you that, though she harbours you as her kinsman, she's nothing allied to your disorders. If you can separate yourself and your misdemeanours, you are welcome to the house; if not, and it would please you to take leave of her, she is very willing to bid you farewell. |
| Toby | (*sings*) 'Farewell, dear heart, since I must needs be gone.' 100 |
| Maria | Nay, good Sir Toby. |
| Feste | (*sings*) 'His eyes do show his days are almost done.' |
| Malv. | Is it even so? |
| Toby | (*sings*) 'But I will never die.' |
| Feste | (*sings*) 'Sir Toby, there you lie.' |
| Malv. | This is much credit to you. |
| Toby | (*sings*) 'Shall I bid him go?' |
| Feste | (*sings*) 'What an if you do?' |

111      **Out . . . lie:** *Sir Toby is about to prove Feste's words wrong. He suddenly becomes savagely serious, stops singing, and attacks Malvolio for exceeding his duties.*

112–114      **because . . . ale:** 'just because you choose to live a sober sort of existence, must everyone else stop enjoying the good things of life?'

115      **ginger:** the spice which was used to add life to both cakes and ale

117–118      **rub . . . crumbs:** 'Go and mind your own business.' (*Malvolio has put on his chain of office over his nightshirt. Sir Toby flicks the chain contemptuously to remind Malvolio that he is only a servant.*)

119–121      **if you . . . rule:** 'if you cared tuppence about keeping on the right side of your mistress, you wouldn't be supplying the drink for this wild party'

122      **by this hand:** a mild oath, appropriate to this prim Puritan (*Malvolio's threat to tell Olivia about Maria is her reason for inventing the plot to get even with him.*)

123      *Maria waits until Malvolio is out of hearing before she calls him an ass, with long ears to shake.*

124–125      **'Twere . . . a-hungry:** *A proverbial way of saying:* 'The best thing to do is . . . .', *although even with a proverb Sir Andrew can still trip himself up and mistake hunger for thirst.*

125–126      **to challenge . . . with him:** 'to challenge him to a fight, and then not to turn up at the appointed place' (*Sir Andrew's very simple plan for revenge is quickly rejected for Maria's more subtle plot. 3.iv shows what a feeble warrior he is.*)

130–131      **she is . . . quiet:** 'she is not herself at all'

131–135      **For Monsieur . . . do it:** 'As for our fine gentleman, Malvolio, leave him to me. If I don't make such a fool of him that everybody will laugh at the mere mention of his name— he'll be the common laughing-stock—then you can think me a complete idiot. I'm certain I know how to do it.'

136      **possess us:** tell us your plan

137      **a kind of Puritan:** *Puritans were extremely unpopular, chiefly because they did their best to spoil most of the popular sports— including theatre-going.*

| | |
|---|---|
| Toby | (*sings*) 'Shall I bid him go, and spare not?' |
| Feste | (*sings*) 'O no, no, no, no, you dare not.' 110 |
| Toby | Out of tune, sir! Ye lie. (*to* Malvolio) Art any more than a steward? Dost thou think, because thou art virtuous, there shall be no more cakes and ale? |
| Feste | Yes, by Saint Anne, and ginger shall be hot in the mouth too. |
| Toby | Thou art in the right. Go, sir, rub your chain with crumbs. A stoup of wine, Maria! |
| Malv. | Mistress Mary, if you prized my lady's favour at any thing more than contempt, you would not 120 give means for this uncivil rule; she shall know of it, by this hand. |

*Exit*

| | |
|---|---|
| Maria | Go, shake your ears! |
| Andrew | 'Twere as good a deed as to drink when a man's a-hungry, to challenge him the field, and then to break promise with him and make a fool of him. |
| Toby | Do it, knight. I'll write thee a challenge; or I'll deliver thy indignation to him by word of mouth. |
| Maria | Sweet Sir Toby, be patient for tonight. Since the youth of the count's was today with my lady, she 130 is much out of quiet. For Monsieur Malvolio, let me alone with him. If I do not gull him into a nayword, and make him a common recreation, do not think I have wit enough to lie straight in my bed. I know I can do it. |
| Toby | Possess us, possess us; tell us something of him. |
| Maria | Marry, sir, sometimes he is a kind of Puritan. |
| Andrew | O, if I thought that, I'd beat him like a dog. |

| | |
|---|---|
| 141 | **exquisite:** precise (*the word bewilders Sir Andrew*) |
| 143–150 | 'He's not much of a Puritan, nor anything for long; he changes his character whenever it seems likely to pay off. He is an affected ass, who learns by heart the sort of things important statesmen say, and then repeats them in great chunks (like bundles of corn). He's got such a high opinion of himself that he is quite convinced that everyone admires him. This weakness of his will give us a marvellous chance to get our revenge.' |
| 152–159 | 'I will drop where he is likely to find them some puzzling love letters, and in them I'll refer to the colour of his beard, the shapeliness of his legs, the way he walks, the look in his eyes, the amount of forehead visible, and the colour of his skin, so that he will see that he is being accurately described. My writing is so like my lady your niece's, that if we come across something one of us has written some time ago and forgotten all about, then we can scarcely tell which of us wrote it.' |
| 161 | *Parrot-like Sir Andrew echoes Sir Toby, as in lines 34 and 55.* |
| 165 | 'That's exactly my idea.' (*a proverbial expression*) |
| 169–173 | 'A joke fit for a king's ears, I promise you. I'm certain my medicine will work on him. I'll show you two where to hide —and Feste here can join you—so that you can see him find the letter and watch how he pieces together the hints I shall put in the letter. But now you'd better go to bed and dream about the likely outcome. Good night.' |
| 169 | **physic:** medicine (*Maria is set to cure Malvolio once and for all of his conceit.*) |

| | |
|---|---|
| Toby | What, for being a Puritan? Thy exquisite reason, dear knight? 140 |
| Andrew | I have no exquisite reason for it, but I have reason good enough. |
| Maria | The devil a Puritan that he is or anything constantly, but a time-pleaser, an affectioned ass that cons state without book, and utters it by great swarths; the best persuaded of himself—so crammed, as he thinks, with excellencies—that it is his ground of faith that all that look on him love him; and on that vice in him will my revenge find notable cause to work. 150 |
| Toby | What wilt thou do? |
| Maria | I will drop in his way some obscure epistles of love; wherein, by the colour of his beard, the shape of his leg, the manner of his gait, the expressure of his eye, forehead and complexion, he shall find himself most feelingly personated. I can write very like my lady, your niece; on a forgotten matter we can hardly make distinction of our hands. |
| Toby | Excellent! I smell a device! 160 |
| Andrew | I have it in my nose too! |
| Toby | He shall think by the letters that thou wilt drop that they come from my niece, and that she's in love with him. |
| Maria | My purpose is indeed a horse of that colour. |
| Toby | And your horse now would make him an ass. |
| Maria | Ass, I doubt not. |
| Andrew | O, 'twill be admirable! |
| Maria | Sport royal, I warrant you! I know my physic will work with him. I will plant you two—and let 170 |

170–171   **let . . . third:** *It is odd that Shakespeare decided that Feste should not, in fact, be present in 2.v and made up the trio with Fabian.*

174   **Penthesilea:** the strongly-built Queen of the Amazons (*Sir Toby is laughing at but also praising the tiny Maria.*)

175   **Before me:** My word!

176   **beagle:** a small hunting dog (*more appropriate to Maria's size*)
  **one that adores me:** *another hint that makes their eventual marriage less of a surprise*

178   *Sir Andrew is not to be outdone; but he speaks rather sadly.*

181–182   'If I can't fix it to marry your niece, I'm going to be awfully out-of-pocket.'

184   **call me 'cut':** insult me as you like

186   **burn some sack:** warm up our drink (*Sack was a cheap Spanish wine, often drunk warm. Characteristically, Sir Toby declines Maria's suggestion that they should go to bed; he says it is hardly worth it now!*)

## Scene 4

The interest in this scene comes almost entirely from the audience's knowing of Viola's secret love for Orsino, and seeing just how near she can come to telling the truth without Orsino understanding. Just for a minute, Orsino is curious about his page-messenger, but then he sinks back into his self-centred love-sickness. It is a surprise to find Feste appearing in Orsino's court, especially since it appears at first that Cesario is being asked to sing (line 3). Shakespeare probably made a late alteration for some reason to do with casting parts, rather than to suggest Feste is a kind of free-lance jester.

1   *Orsino calls in his small group of court musicians to revive the mood of the play's opening scene. A sadly romantic melody is played until Feste enters.*

3   **but:** 'just let's hear'

5–7   'It seemed to soothe away my suffering far better than these trivial and unnatural modern tunes, which are part and parcel of our modern craving for speed at all costs.' (*Orsino*

the fool make a third—where he shall find the
letter; observe his construction of it. For this
night, to bed, and dream on the event! Farewell!

*Exit*

| | |
|---|---|
| Toby | Good night, Penthesilea! |
| Andrew | Before me, she's a good wench! |
| Toby | She's a beagle true-bred, and one that adores me; what of that? |
| Andrew | I was adored once too. |
| Toby | Let's to bed, knight. Thou hadst need send for more money. |
| Andrew | If we cannot recover your niece, I am a foul way out. |
| Toby | Send for money, knight; if thou hast her not in the end, call me 'cut'. |
| Andrew | If I do not, never trust me; take it how you will. |
| Toby | Come, come, I'll go burn some sack; 'tis too late to go to bed now. Come, knight; come, knight. |

180

*Exeunt*


SCENE 4   Orsino's palace
*Enter* Duke, Viola, Curio *and attendants.*

Duke    Give me some music.

*Enter musicians*

Now, good morrow, friends.
    Now, good Cesario, but that piece of song,
That old and antique song we heard last night.
Methought it did relieve my passion much,
More than light airs and recollected terms
Of these most brisk and giddy-paced times.

*is one of those people who look back sadly to an age of romance, like the imaginary world of King Arthur. Hence his preference for old-fashioned music.)*

12     *Feste seems to have little use in Olivia's household; he too is a relic of the past, when times were happier under Olivia's father.*

16–21     *Orsino is posing as the true lover; let others compare their love with his to see if theirs is genuine. The irony is that his 'suffering' seems almost comical compared with Viola's. Here she is, pining for this man, and not able to tell a soul.*

19–21     'Lovers are firm-minded in one matter only: they are devoted to the person they love. In every other matter they are unbalanced and unpredictable.'

22–23     'It describes perfectly what the heart feels' (*Viola's emotional response to the music at once attracts Orsino's admiration, just as her outbursts of genuine feeling attracted Olivia.*)

26     **Hath . . . favour:** 'Has been attracted to someone's face'

28     **by your favour:** 'if it please you' *and* 'on your face' (*By a series of answers which mean one thing to Orsino, and another to the audience and herself, Viola avoids telling a lie about her own feelings.*)

30     **complexion:** general appearance

33–39     'Then she's too old for you. Let a woman always marry a man older than herself. Then she will grow like him in her ways, and continue to hold his affection. For, however much we flatter ourselves, boy, the truth is that our love is more fickle and unreliable than a woman's. We fall more desperately in love, we hesitate, we quickly exhaust our passion and see it fade away—all more rapidly than any woman.' (*Orsino is confessing the weakness of a man's love, that its passion is quickly exhausted. He is being unusually realistic for him and also, without knowing it, advising Viola to choose a husband of about his age.*)

|  |  |  |
|---|---|---|
|  | Come, but one verse. | |
| Curio | He is not here, so please your lordship, that should sing it. | 10 |
| Duke | Who was it? | |
| Curio | Feste the jester, my lord—a fool that the Lady Olivia's father took much delight in. He is about the house. | |
| Duke | Seek him out, and play the tune the while. | |

*Exit* Curio

*The musicians play*

|  |  |  |
|---|---|---|
|  | Come hither, boy. If ever thou shalt love,<br>In the sweet pangs of it remember me;<br>For, such as I am, all true lovers are,<br>Unstaid and skittish in all motions else,<br>Save in the constant image of the creature<br>That is beloved. How dost thou like this tune? | 20 |
| Viola | It gives a very echo to the seat<br>Where love is throned. | |
| Duke | Thou dost speak masterly.<br>My life upon it, young though thou art, thine eye<br>Hath stayed upon some favour that it loves;<br>Hath it not, boy? | |
| Viola | A little, by your favour. | |
| Duke | What kind of woman is it? | |
| Viola | Of your complexion. | 30 |
| Duke | She is not worth thee, then. What years, in faith? | |
| Viola | About your years, my lord. | |
| Duke | Too old, by heaven! Let still the woman take<br>An elder than herself; so wears she to him,<br>So sways she level in her husband's heart. | |

42      'Or your love will gradually slacken' (*like a bow which is kept drawn taut*)

45–46   *Viola sadly agrees that it is a tragedy how quickly a woman's beauty fades.*

47      *While Feste arranges with the musicians to accompany his song, Orsino tells Cesario how this song reminds him of a simple innocent life long ago, so different from the modern hectic world of the court. The music is his way of escaping from his responsibilities as a Duke.*

49–54   'It is a song that used to be sung by the women who spin and knit sitting at the doors of their cottages enjoying the sun, and by carefree girls making lace with bobbins made of bone; it tells the simple truth and lightly touches upon innocent love; it's a bit of the old world.'

57      *This song is in a completely different mood from Feste's first song. Its picture of a lover welcoming the thought of death fits the melancholy Orsino. He is in the mood for saying that he is* 'slain by a fair cruel maid' *called Olivia.*

57      **Come away:** Come to me

58      **sad cypress:** a coffin made of dark cypress wood, the tree which often grew in churchyards

59      **fie away, breath:** away with life

61      **stuck all with yew:** decorated with pieces of yew (*the other tree associated with graveyards*)

63–64   *Like Orsino, the imaginary lover in this song believes that there was never a lover who died for love so faithful as himself—an odd contradiction of Orsino's confession in lines 37-39.*

|       |                                                          |    |
|-------|----------------------------------------------------------|----|
|       | For, boy, however we do praise ourselves,                |    |
|       | Our fancies are more giddy and unfirm,                   |    |
|       | More longing, wavering, sooner lost and worn,            |    |
|       | Than women's are.                                        |    |
| Viola | I think it well, my lord.                                | 40 |
| Duke  | Then let thy love be younger than thyself,               |    |
|       | Or thy affection cannot hold the bent.                   |    |
|       | For women are as roses, whose fair flower,               |    |
|       | Being once displayed, doth fall that very hour.          |    |
| Viola | And so they are; alas, that they are so!                 |    |
|       | To die, even when they to perfection grow!               |    |

*Enter* Curio *and* Feste

| Duke  | O fellow, come; the song we had last night.              |    |
|-------|----------------------------------------------------------|----|
|       | Mark it, Cesario, it is old and plain;                   |    |
|       | The spinsters and the knitters in the sun,               |    |
|       | And the free maids that weave their thread with bones,   | 50 |
|       | Do use to chant it; it is silly sooth,                   |    |
|       | And dallies with the innocence of love,                  |    |
|       | Like the old age.                                        |    |
| Feste | Are you ready, sir?                                      |    |
| Duke  | Ay, prithee sing.                                        |    |

*The musicians play the introduction*

| Feste | (*sings*) Come away, come away, death,                   |    |
|-------|----------------------------------------------------------|----|
|       | And in sad cypress let me be laid.                       |    |
|       | Fie away, fie away, breath,                              |    |
|       | I am slain by a fair cruel maid.                         | 60 |
|       | My shroud of white, stuck all with yew,                  |    |
|       | O, prepare it.                                           |    |
|       | My part of death, no one so true                         |    |
|       | Did share it.                                            |    |

77–78    *Light-heartedly, Feste quotes the proverb meaning that you never get pleasure for nothing.*

79    *Orsino is not in the mood for idle chatter; the song has returned his thoughts to Olivia; so he, most politely, dismisses Feste. Feste, playfully yet half seriously, grumbles about Orsino not knowing his own mind—one minute in one mood, and the next in a quite different one.*

80    **the melancholy god:** Saturn, the god whose planet was supposed to cause the fashionable disease of melancholy, a kind of permanent depression

81    **changeable taffeta:** shot silk which reflects many colours (*It would be a help, Feste says, if Orsino wore a sign to show everyone how changeable he is.*)

82    **opal:** a precious stone which shows different colours as you turn it round

82–86    **I would have . . . nothing:** 'Men who are as changeable as you should go to sea, for, if your business was always changing and you didn't mind where you went, then you would be perfectly satisfied to come back empty-handed. (*Feste compares Orsino's mind to a 'tramp' ship, which picks up cargoes here and there, and has no fixed destination or route.*)

87–95    'The rest of you may go. Now, Cesario, go once again to that cruel queen; tell her that my love is not greedy like other people's and has not the slightest interest in her paltry estates. I care as little for the lands and wealth she has been lucky enough to inherit, as I care for Lady Luck herself. No, it is her dazzlingly rare beauty, in which Nature has dressed her, that has fired me with love.' (*Orsino cannot believe Olivia may not love him; so he thinks of other possible explanations for her conduct. Perhaps she thinks he is after her property—* 'quantity of dirty lands'.)

89    **sovereign cruelty:** *Orsino's phrase recalls the 'fair cruel maid' of the song.*

Not a flower, not a flower sweet,
　　On my black coffin let there be strown;
Not a friend, not a friend greet
　　My poor corpse, where my bones shall be
　　　thrown.
A thousand thousand sighs to save,　　　　　70
　　　Lay me, O, where
Sad true lover never find my grave,
　　　To weep there.

Duke　　There's for thy pains.

Feste　　No pains, sir; I take pleasure in singing, sir.

Duke　　I'll pay thy pleasure then.

Feste　　Truly, sir, and pleasure will be paid one time or another.

Duke　　Give me now leave to leave thee.

Feste　　Now the melancholy god protect thee, and the　80
tailor make thy doublet of changeable taffeta,
for thy mind is a very opal! I would have men of
such constancy put to sea, that their business
might be everything and their intent everywhere;
for that's it that always makes a good voyage of
nothing. Farewell!

　　　　　　　　　　　　　　　　　*Exit*

Duke　　Let all the rest give place.

　　　　　　　　　　*Exeunt all but* Duke *and* Viola

　　Once more, Cesario,
Get thee to yond same sovereign cruelty;
Tell her my love, more noble than the world,　　90
Prizes not quantity of dirty lands;
The parts that fortune hath bestowed upon her,
Tell her I hold as giddily as fortune;

98      *Orsino is incapable of taking no for an answer, but Viola knows from personal experience that some lovers have to.*

103–113   'A woman's heart wouldn't be able to stand the pressure of love that my heart endures.' (*Orsino forgets his praise of women's ability to sustain their love.*) 'You couldn't find one large enough to contain such a volume of love; their hearts are not made to sustain really deep love. To be honest, it's not love that a woman feels but a kind of appetite—it's nothing to do with the heart, really, It's an appetite that can have its fill of love, then find the taste unpleasant, so unpleasant that it is sick; whereas it would be impossible to fully satisfy my love—it's like the sea always hungering for more. Don't try to compare any love a woman might have for me with the feeling I have for Olivia—there's no comparison.' (*This is Orsino's last appearance before the final scene of the play, and this is his last long speech. It leaves the memory of Orsino arrogantly sweeping aside the thought of any woman being able to rival his passionate love.*)

108      **liver:** *Elizabethans thought the origin of love was in the liver. The heart became affected later.*

114–120   *Viola, forgetting her disguise, is about to tell Orsino about her own love, when she suddenly realises and stops abruptly. Orsino, surprised at being contradicted, asks her to continue, but this gives Viola the chance to change what she was going to say. Her imaginary sister is her way of talking of herself. Again she cleverly avoids having to tell a direct lie.*

116      'I know to my cost what love a woman can feel for a man.'

121      'What became of her?'

122–131   'Nothing came of it, my lord; she never revealed her love; instead, she kept it a secret and so pined away, just as a canker curled up in a rose-bud eats away the red and white rose petals. She sank into a state of deep depression and sat sadly smiling in her sorrow, like a carving on a tombstone of a girl waiting calmly, as though she were Patience itself. Surely you would admit that this was true love? We men probably talk more about our love and swear great oaths about it, but we say far more than we are prepared to do; we are always great ones for swearing undying love, but we do little when it comes to proving our love.' (*Viola exaggerates*

|        | But 'tis that miracle and queen of gems, |
|        | That nature pranks her in, attracts my soul. |
| Viola  | But if she cannot love you, sir? |
| Duke   | I cannot be so answered. |
| Viola  | Sooth, but you must. |
|        | Say that some lady—as perhaps there is— |
|        | Hath for your love as great a pang of heart  100 |
|        | As you have for Olivia; you cannot love her; |
|        | You tell her so; must she not then be answered? |
| Duke   | There is no woman's sides |
|        | Can bide the beating of so strong a passion |
|        | As love doth give my heart; no woman's heart |
|        | So big, to hold so much—they lack retention. |
|        | Alas, their love may be called appetite— |
|        | No motion of the liver but the palate— |
|        | That suffers surfeit, cloyment and revolt; |
|        | But mine is all as hungry as the sea,  110 |
|        | And can digest as much. Make no compare |
|        | Between that love a woman can bear me |
|        | And that I owe Olivia. |
| Viola  | Ay, but I know— |
| Duke   | What dost thou know? |
| Viola  | Too well what love women to men may owe. |
|        | In faith, they are as true of heart as we. |
|        | My father had a daughter loved a man, |
|        | As it might be, perhaps, were I a woman, |
|        | I should your lordship.  120 |
| Duke   | And what's her history? |
| Viola  | A blank, my lord. She never told her love, |
|        | But let concealment like a worm in the bud |
|        | Feed on her damask cheek; she pined in thought |
|        | And, with a green and yellow melancholy, |

the idea of a girl pining for love, so that the audience can see by
comparison both how bravely she faces up to exactly the same predica-
ment as her fake sister and how shallow is Orsino's love.)

125 **green and yellow:** the sickly colours appropriate to the
mood

134–135 *Viola realises that Orsino will quickly see through her riddle, and so
swiftly changes the subject to Olivia.*

136 **that's the theme:** that's what we should be thinking about

138 **can give no place:** cannot be put to one side
**denay:** denial

## Scene 5

An Elizabethan or a modern audience would require only a
few shrubs to suggest Olivia's garden. The scene's fun
depends upon the three eavesdroppers being seen and
heard by the audience, but not by Malvolio, as they hide
behind the low box-tree, something like a privet hedge.
Malvolio's folly in this scene is similar to, but more comical
than, Orsino's; both have convinced themselves that Olivia
must find them irresistible.

1 **Come thy ways:** Come with me (*Sir Toby is soon to need
some help in staging the 'fight' between Sir Andrew and Viola, so
this is a good chance to bring a new companion, Fabian, into the
plot.*)

2 **a scruple:** the smallest part

3 **melancholy:** *As a contrast to Orsino, Fabian considers this
disease would be a comical kind of punishment in his own case.*

5 **sheep-biter:** fault-finder (*like a dog snapping at sheep*)
**come . . . shame:** 'see Malvolio thoroughly disgraced'

6–7 *Fabian's reason for disliking Malvolio is that the steward sneaked
to Olivia about Fabian's arranging a bear-baiting session in her
garden.*

8 **have the bear again:** *Sir Toby's and Maria's plan is to bait
Malvolio almost as though he were a bear tied to a stake and attacked
by dogs; by the time they are finished with him he will feel he has
been beaten 'black and blue'.*

11 'If we don't, we shan't deserve to go on living.'

She sat like patience on a monument,
Smiling at grief. Was not this love indeed?
   We men may say more, swear more; but
indeed
Our shows are more than will; for still we prove   130
Much in our vows but little in our love.

Duke        But died thy sister of her love, my boy?

Viola       I am all the daughters of my father's house,
And all the brothers too; and yet I know not—
Sir, shall I to this lady?

Duke        Ay, that's the theme;
To her in haste. Give her this jewel. Say,
My love can give no place, bide no denay.

                                     *Exeunt*


SCENE 5   Olivia's garden

*Enter* Sir Toby, Sir Andrew *and* Fabian.


Toby       Come thy ways, Signior Fabian.

Fabian    Nay, I'll come; if I lose a scruple of this sport, let
me be boiled to death with melancholy.

Toby       Wouldst thou not be glad to have the niggardly,
rascally sheep-biter come by some notable shame?

Fabian    I would exult, man. You know he brought me out
of favour with my lady about a bear-baiting here.

Toby       To anger him we'll have the bear again, and we
will fool him black and blue; shall we not, Sir
Andrew?                                    10

Andrew   An we do not, it is pity of our lives.

12–13    **my metal of India**: my precious girl (*India was the supposed source of fabulous wealth.*)

14    *Maria hustles the three conspirators out of sight.*

15–17    *Maria has been watching Malvolio strutting up and down, looking at his shadow as he copies the walk and flourishing gestures of courtiers.*

18–19    **contemplative idiot**: a fool completely wrapped up in his dream-world

19    **Close**: Keep out of sight (*said to Sir Toby and the others*)

23    *It is some 50 lines—about two minutes' acting time—before Malvolio spots the letter. In this time he makes it fully clear that he thinks he stands a good chance of marrying Olivia; the letter only confirms his conceited opinion.*

23    **fortune**: *more than 'luck'; Malvolio believes Olivia is 'destined' to be his.*

24    **affect**: care for (*Maria has laid the groundwork for her plan by dropping hints to Malvolio.*)

24–28    **I have heard . . . on it**: 'She has almost said as much to me herself when she said that, if ever she should fall in love, the man she chose would look like me. Besides, she treats me far less like a servant than she does any other of those that serve her. So how else am I to interpret her words and behaviour?'

29    *As Malvolio struts up and down the stage, deep in his day-dream, the three listeners have great difficulty in controlling themselves. They keep forgetting that they are supposed to be in hiding, as they are alternately furious at Malvolio's colossal conceit, and delighted at the success of their plan.*

29    **overweening**: cocksure

30–32    'Not so loud. He's just like a turkey the way he struts about. Look how he's parading as if he were someone of importance!'

33    **'Slight**: *A mild oath—a corruption of 'By God's light'. Sir Andrew sounds very aggressive, until it actually comes to fighting!*

*Enter* Maria

Toby    Here comes the little villain. How now, my metal
        of India?

Maria   Get ye all three into the box-tree. Malvolio's
        coming down this walk; he has been yonder in
        the sun practising behaviour to his own shadow
        this half hour. Observe him for the love of
        mockery, for I know this letter will make a con-
        templative idiot of him. Close, in the name of
        jesting! Lie thou there (*throws down a letter*), for    20
        here comes the trout that must be caught with
        tickling.

                                                        *Exit*

*Enter* Malvolio

Malv.   'Tis but fortune; all is fortune. Maria once told
        me she did affect me, and I have heard herself
        come thus near, that, should she fancy, it should
        be one of my complexion. Besides, she uses me
        with a more exalted respect than anyone else
        that follows her. What should I think on it?

Toby    Here's an overweening rogue!

Fabian  O, peace! Contemplation makes a rare turkey-     30
        cock of him. How he jets under his advanced
        plumes!

Andrew  'Slight, I could so beat the rogue!

Toby    Peace, I say!

Malv.   To be Count Malvolio!

Toby    Ah, rogue!

Andrew  Pistol him! Pistol him!

Toby    Peace, peace!

85

40    **yeoman of the wardrobe:** a servant in charge of his
      master's clothes (*Malvolio finds hope in the example of a lady
      marrying beneath her rank.*)

41    **Jezebel:** *Sir Andrew, confused as usual, has little reason for
      calling Malvolio the notoriously evil queen in the Old Testament.*

42–43  'Now he's really fallen into our trap. Just look how pompous
      his imagination makes him.'

45    **my state:** official chair, from which he could issue orders to
      the household

46    **stone-bow:** cross-bow for shooting down troublesome birds

47–49  'Summoning the servants to me as I wear my gown of rich
      velvet, patterned with some leafy design; having just got up
      from the couch where Olivia is still lying asleep.' (*Malvolio
      can see it all so clearly in his mind's eye that he even knows the
      material he will choose for his gown. This is the one glimpse of
      Olivia in his pictured world; he is far more interested in the chance
      of lording it over the servants.*)

50    *A more vivid way of saying*: 'Hell and damnation!'

52–55  'Then to act like a king on his throne, and, after gazing round
      solemnly at the assembled servants, to let them see I know
      who is boss and to remind them of their inferior status, to
      ask someone where cousin Toby is' (*The thought of his being
      related to, and so on an equal social footing with, Sir Toby delights
      Malvolio, and infuriates Sir Toby so much that he wants to lock the
      man away.*)

58–59  **make out for him:** rush to fetch him

60–61  **play . . . jewel:** *Malvolio is acting the part, as he imagines the
      scene. He starts to play casually with his steward's chain of office, then
      realises he will have discarded such things, and so quickly replaces it
      in his mind, by a more glamorous gold chain with a rich jewel on it.*

61    **courtesies:** bows respectfully

63–64  'Do be quiet—even though it's torture, like being strung
      between two chariots driven in opposite directions, to force
      us to speak.'

65–66  'I stretch out my hand for him to take, like this (*Malvolio
      demonstrates the lordly gesture*), restraining the smile I would
      give to a relative by adopting the severe expression of a man
      in authority—' (*Malvolio's language is pompous—in keeping with
      the imaginary occasion.*)

69–71  'Saying, "Dear Toby, since I have had the good fortune to

| Malv. | There is example for it; the Lady of the Strachy married the yeoman of the wardrobe. | 40 |
| Andrew | Fie on him! Jezebel! | |
| Fabian | O, peace! Now he's deeply in. Look how imagination blows him. | |
| Malv. | Having been three months married to her, sitting in my state— | |
| Toby | O for a stone-bow to hit him in the eye! | |
| Malv. | Calling my officers about me, in my branched velvet gown; having come from a day-bed, where I have left Olivia sleeping— | |
| Toby | Fire and brimstone! | 50 |
| Fabian | O, peace, peace! | |
| Malv. | And then to have the humour of state; and, after a demure travel of regard, telling them I know my place as I would they should do theirs, to ask for my kinsman Toby— | |
| Toby | Bolts and shackles! | |
| Fabian | O, peace, peace, peace! Now, now! | |
| Malv. | Seven of my people with an obedient start make out for him; I frown the while, and perchance wind up my watch or play with my—some rich jewel; Toby approaches, courtesies there to me— | 60 |
| Toby | Shall this fellow live? | |
| Fabian | Though our silence be drawn from us with cars, yet peace! | |
| Malv. | I extend my hand to him thus, quenching my familiar smile with an austere regard of control— | |
| Toby | And does not Toby take you a blow on the lips, then? | |
| Malv. | Saying, 'Cousin Toby, my fortunes having cast | |

marry your niece, I have the right to speak to you like this—" '

74    'Why, the miserable creature!' (*as unpleasant and unwanted as a* 'scab')

75    'Do be quiet, or we'll spoil the best part of the trick.' (*Malvolio has still to see the letter.*)

76    **treasure:** the most valuable part

78    *Sir Andrew eagerly shows that he also understands what Malvolio is saying. Fortunately, his 'friends' are too absorbed to take advantage of this admission of his folly.*

81    'What's this? Something of interest?'

82    'Now the bird is practically in the trap.' (*The woodcock was thought of as a stupid bird.*)

83–84    'If only he takes it into his head to read the letter aloud' (*Sir Toby is bursting with curiosity to know what is in the letter.*)

86–87    **C's; U's; T's; P's:** *The letters themselves have no secret message apart from the crude humour.* 'Cut' *is the word Sir Toby used as an insult in 2.iii.184, and Sir Andrew's spelling it out again makes sure that the audience does not miss the joke.*

85    **this is . . . hand:** 'it's her handwriting all right; it would be crazy to doubt it.'

90–91    *Malvolio reads out the mysterious inscriptions on the outside of the letter, never pauses to consider it may be none of his business, but affectedly apologises to the sealing wax for breaking it open. Then he notices the wax carries the impression—'impressure'—left by Olivia's ring and this makes him quite certain that Olivia has written it.*

93    **Lucrece:** *Olivia's signet ring has engraved on it the head of the famous tragic Roman wife. It is in keeping with how Olivia sees herself at the beginning of the play as a lady cast in a tragic role.*

95    'He'll swallow this now, hook, line and sinker.'

100–101    **What . . . altered?:** *Eager to see what comes next, Malvolio glances at the next part of the message where the verse form,* 'numbers', *is different. Then he pauses to think how marvellous it would be if this note perhaps was meant for him.*

|         | me on your niece, give me this prerogative of speech—' | 70 |
|---------|--------------------------------------------------------|----|
| Toby    | What, what? | |
| Malv.   | 'You must amend your drunkenness.' | |
| Toby    | Out, scab! | |
| Fabian  | Nay, patience, or we break the sinews of our plot. | |
| Malv.   | 'Besides, you waste the treasure of your time, with a foolish knight.' | |
| Andrew  | That's me, I warrant you. | |
| Malv.   | 'One Sir Andrew—' | |
| Andrew  | I knew 'twas I, for many do call me fool. | 80 |
| Malv.   | (*seeing the letter*) What employment have we here? | |
| Fabian  | Now is the woodcock near the gin. | |
| Toby    | O, peace! And the spirit of humours intimate reading aloud to him! | |
| Malv.   | By my life, this is my lady's hand; these be her very C's, her U's, and her T's, and thus makes she her great P's. It is, in contempt of question, her hand. | |
| Andrew  | Her C's, her U's, and her T's; why that? | |
| Malv.   | (*reads*) *To the unknown beloved, this, and my good wishes.* | 90 |
|         | Her very phrases! By your leave, wax. Soft! And the impressure her Lucrece, with which she uses to seal. 'Tis my lady! To whom should this be? | |
| Fabian  | This wins him, liver and all. | |
| Malv.   | *Jove knows I love,* | |
|         | *But who?* | |
|         | *Lips do not move,* | |
|         | *No man must know.* | |
|         | '*No man must know.*' What follows, the numbers | 100 |

103 **brock:** badger (*yet one more of the many unflattering comparisons of Malvolio to various animals*)

104–105 *The first hint that Olivia is the supposed writer, one who is forced by her position to give orders to the man she secretly loves.*

105 **a Lucrece knife:** *a knife such as Lucretia used to kill herself*

106 *The melodrama of this line hardly suggests Olivia's hand, but Malvolio is already 'hooked'. Even Fabian considers it pretty corny stuff, 'fustian'.*

112 **dressed:** prepared

113 'How keen the hawk is to swoop off after the wrong bird!' (*that is, Malvolio is on the wrong scent*)

115–119 **Why this ... in me:** 'The meaning is obvious to any man with the least intelligence. There is no difficulty there. But what about this end bit? What does the arrangement of these letters suggest? If only I could make it refer to me in some way.' (*There seems little reason for Maria's rearrangement of the letters, except it allows Malvolio to prove how clever he is at a puzzle, and allows Sir Toby and Fabian a few puns.*)

121 **at a cold scent:** baffled (*like a hound, called Sowter, who cannot pick up the scent*)

122–123 'The hound will yelp that it has found the scent even though it's the wrong scent—even if it stinks of fox.'

125–126 **The cur ... faults:** 'This dog's very good at picking up breaks in the scent.'

128 **that ... probation:** 'the rest of the letters are not consistent; it's all wrong when you try to work it out.'

130 *Fabian thinks of Malvolio's wail of misery when he learns the truth.*

altered? 'No man must know.' If this should be thee, Malvolio!

Toby   Marry, hang thee, brock!

Malv.
> *I may command where I adore,*
> *But silence, like a Lucrece knife,*
> *With bloodless stroke my heart doth gore;*
> *M.O.A.I. doth sway my life.*

Fabian   A fustian riddle!

Toby   Excellent wench, say I.

Malv.   '*M.O.A.I. doth sway my life*' Nay, but first let me 110 see, let me see, let me see.

Fabian   What dish of poison has she dressed him!

Toby   And with what wing the staniel checks at it!

Malv.   '*I may command where I adore*'—why, she may command me; I serve her, she is my lady. Why this is evident to any formal capacity. There is no obstruction in this. And the end—what should that alphabetical position portend? If I could make that resemble something in me! Softly! '*M.O.A.I.*'   120

Toby   O ay, make up that! He is now at a cold scent.

Fabian   Sowter will cry upon it for all this, though it be as rank as a fox.

Malv.   '*M*'—Malvolio! '*M*'—why, that begins my name!

Fabian   Did not I say he would work it out? The cur is excellent at faults.

Malv.   '*M*'—but then there is no consonancy in the sequel; that suffers under probation. '*A*' should follow, but '*O*' does.

Fabian   And '*O*' shall end, I hope!   130

Toby   Ay, or I'll cudgel him and make him cry '*O*!'

133–135    'If you could see behind your back, you would see what ridicule there is in store for you, and how little good fortune' (*The pun from Fabian as he peeps out behind Malvolio's back is almost inviting Malvolio to turn round.*)

136–137    **This . . . to me:** 'The disguised meaning isn't as obvious as it was in the bits of verse, but with a little effort it could be made to refer to me.'

140    *Maria's letter is comical (because of the way it uses oddly contrasting tones: romantic exaggeration, down-to-earth instructions, moralising and nagging), but not crude (because it produces neatly balanced phrases and rhythmically impressive sentences).*

140–154    'If you find this letter, then consider this. By reason of my birth I am your superior, but don't let this put you off. There are some people who are born great, and others who work their way up, but there are also some who are made a free gift of greatness. Take the chance now offered to you; commit yourself body and soul, and start behaving like the man you could easily become. Throw away your humbleness, like a snake shedding its useless skin, and appear a new man. Boldly confront a relative, and put up with no nonsense from the servants. Learn the jargon of politicians (to impress people with your learning) and adopt some way of behaving that will set you apart from the common herd of men. Have you forgotten who it was who admired your yellow stockings and said she would like you always to wear cross-gartering? Have you forgotten? Well then, what are you waiting for? Your fortune's made, if that's what you want; if you don't, then you had better remain a servant for the rest of your life, fit only to associate with servants, and unfit even to toy with the good fortune that might be yours. Adieu, from your lady who would willingly reverse her role (*whereby she would become Malvolio's "servant" in love and he would be her "lord"*).' (*Maria is trying to provoke him to overstep his authority which put him in charge of Olivia's servants only. The old-fashioned gaudy colour of his stockings and the style of fastening the garters above and below the knee and tying the ends in a large bow would at once cause Malvolio to be laughed at.*)

155    *Love letters and love poetry are very fond of such contradictions. The lady is 'unhappy' because her love is so far unreturned; but 'fortunate' because she is in love with such a marvellous man.*

156–169    'The meaning of this is obvious; it's as plain as a stretch of

| | |
|---|---|
| Malv. | And then '*I*' comes behind. |
| Fabian | Ay, an you had any eye behind you, you might see more detraction at your heels than fortunes before you. |
| Malv. | '*M.O.A.I.*' This simulation is not as the former, and yet to crush this a little, it would bow to me, for every one of these letters are in my name. Soft, here follows prose: |

*If this fall into thy hand, revolve. In my stars I am above* 140
*thee, but be not afraid of greatness; some are born great,*
*some achieve greatness, and some have greatness thrust*
*upon them. Thy fates open their hands; let thy blood*
*and spirit embrace them; and, to inure thyself to what*
*thou art like to be, cast thy humble slough and appear*
*fresh. Be opposite with a kinsman, surly with servants;*
*let thy tongue tang arguments of state; put thyself into*
*the trick of singularity. She thus advises thee that sighs*
*for thee. Remember who commended thy yellow stockings,*
*and wished to see thee ever cross-gartered; I say, remem-* 150
*ber. Go to! Thou art made if thou desirest to be so; if*
*not, let me see thee a steward still, the fellow of servants,*
*and not worthy to touch fortune's fingers. Farewell. She*
*that would alter services with thee,*

*The Fortunate-Unhappy.*

Daylight and champain discovers not more—this
is open! I will be proud, I will read politic authors,
I will baffle Sir Toby, I will wash off gross
acquaintance, I will be point-devise the very man.
I do not now fool myself to let imagination jade 160
me; for every reason excites to this, that my lady
loves me. She did commend my yellow stockings
of late, she did praise my leg being cross-gartered,
and in this she manifests herself to my love, and

open country ('champain') seen in broad daylight. I will be proud; I'll read books about politics; I'll publicly disgrace Sir Toby; I'll discard any friends who are beneath my social status; I will become the perfect gentleman in every particular. I'm not kidding myself this time or letting my imagination fool me. Every piece of evidence fires me with the certainty that my lady loves me. It is true that recently she admired my yellow stockings and the cross-gartering I was wearing. That must have been her way of showing her love for me, and now she is setting me this lover's task by commanding me to dress the way she likes me. I thank the gods who have made me so happy. All right, I will be aloof and resolute, and I will wear yellow stockings and cross-gartering in just so much time as it takes me to put them on.'
(*Like Orsino and Olivia, Malvolio makes a fool of himself by believing the world is as he wishes it would be and not as it really is. With his affected references to the gods or some kindly planet, Malvolio, Olivia's supposedly wise old adviser, behaves like an infatuated young man thanking the stars for his good fortune.*)

172    *The most obvious way to make Malvolio appear mad is to have him smiling for no apparent reason.*

172    **entertainest:** accept

173    **still:** always

175    **I will smile:** *Malvolio pulls horrible faces as he goes out practising some unaccustomed smiles.*

177    *The three conspirators have been cramped all this while behind their box-tree. They now emerge and caper delightedly about the stage.*

178    **Sophy:** Shah of Persia, renowned for his wealth

179    *Another hint as to what to expect at the end of the play.*

184    **gull:** fool

185    *Sir Toby is prepared to reward Maria with whatever she wishes; he will even grovel before her like a conquered general before his conqueror. Sir Andrew can do nothing but, parrot-like, imitate Sir Toby.*

187–188    'Shall we play dice with my freedom at stake, and if you throw the winning three then I'll be your slave?'

190–192    'You have filled his head with such a wild dream that when he realises the truth he will go mad.' (*Sir Toby looks forward gleefully to the moment Malvolio sees he's been fooled.*)

193    *Maria is eager to hear how successful her plot has been, and at last gets a word in.*

with a kind of injunction drives me to these habits of her liking. I thank my stars; I am happy! I will be strange, stout, in yellow stockings and cross-gartered, even with the swiftness of putting on. Jove and my stars be praised!

Here is yet a postscript.                                          170

*Thou canst not choose but know who I am. If thou entertainest my love, let it appear in thy smiling; thy smiles become thee well. Therefore in my presence still smile, dear my sweet, I prithee.*

Jove, I thank thee! I will smile. I will do everything that thou wilt have me.

*Exit*

| | |
|---|---|
| Fabian | I will not give my part of this sport for a pension of thousands to be paid from the Sophy. |
| Toby | I could marry this wench for this device. |
| Andrew | So could I too.                                          180 |
| Toby | And ask no other dowry with her but such another jest. |
| Andrew | Nor I neither. |

*Enter* Maria

| | |
|---|---|
| Fabian | Here comes my noble gull-catcher. |
| Toby | Wilt thou set thy foot on my neck? |
| Andrew | Or on mine either? |
| Toby | Shall I play my freedom at trey-trip, and become thy bond-slave? |
| Andrew | In faith, or I either? |
| Toby | Why, thou hast put him in such a dream that, 190 when the image of it leaves him, he must run mad. |
| Maria | Nay, but say true, does it work upon him? |

194     **aqua-vitae:** brandy (*midwives were proverbial heavy-drinkers*)

196–203     *Maria explains, what might have been guessed, that the instructions she inserted in the letter related to dress and behaviour which were particularly objectionable to Olivia. She then bustles the men away to see the next stage of Malvolio's undoing.*

200     **addicted to:** given up to

201     **melancholy:** *Olivia's 'illness' is here identified with Orsino's by giving it the same name. This is the result of Viola's visit, not Olivia's original grief for her brother.*

202     **a notable contempt:** a notorious figure of fun

204     **Tartar:** Tartarus, a region of hell

| | |
|---|---|
| Toby | Like aqua-vitæ with a midwife. |
| Maria | If you will then see the fruits of the sport, mark his first approach before my lady. He will come to her in yellow stockings, and 'tis a colour she abhors, and cross-gartered, a fashion she detests; and he will smile upon her, which will now be so unsuitable to her disposition—being addicted to 200 a melancholy as she is—that it cannot but turn him into a notable contempt. If you will see it, follow me. |
| Toby | To the gates of Tartar, thou most excellent devil of wit! |
| Andrew | I'll make one too. |

*Exeunt*

This scene involves Viola in a continuous battle of wits. First, she has to parry Feste's assault of puns and quibbles, which were the usual weapons of a professional jester. Then, more seriously, she has to remain dignified yet apparently cold-hearted when Olivia declares her love for this attractive young 'man', Cesario. It is hard for us today to understand and so enjoy fully the humour of the first part, though it is easy to share Feste's delight in his own cleverness. The pathos of the second part is achieved if we sympathise with the two girls in their very awkward situation.

1   **Save thee:** God save thee

2   **tabor:** small drum

3   **by:** *Feste deliberately misunderstands this to mean 'near', not 'by means of'.*

4   **churchman:** clergyman

8   **lies by:** 'lives near' *and* 'sleeps with' (*Viola quickly answers quibble with quibble.*)

9   **stands by:** 'stands next to' *and* 'is supported by'

11–13   'You have made your point, young sir. What a clever lot we are these days! A quick-witted man treats a serious remark ('sentence') like a kid leather ('cheveril') glove—in next to no time he has turned it inside out.' (*Feste pretends to be critically judging the age, but he himself makes his living by twisting the meaning of words. This chatter is not altogether out of place in a play which concerns so many people who are not what they seem.*)

14–15   'Certainly, people who play cunningly with words may soon make them so loose in meaning as to be almost meaningless.' (*The word 'wanton' provides Feste with an obvious chance for a bawdy joke.*)

18   **dally with:** 'play with the meaning of' *and* 'carelessly make love to'

19   **wanton:** 'lack her good reputation' *and* 'a prostitute' ('wanton' *and* 'want one'—*i.e.* 'lack a name'—*would sound nearly the same in Elizabethan times*)

20–21   **words ... them:** 'words are worthless, now that men cannot be trusted to do what they say and so have to use written contracts ('bonds')'

23   **Troth:** Indeed

# ACT 3

SCENE 1    Outside Olivia's house
*Enter* Viola, *and* Feste *playing his pipe and tabor.*

| | |
|---|---|
| Viola | Save thee, friend, and thy music. Dost thou live by thy tabor? |
| Feste | No, sir, I live by the church. |
| Viola | Art thou a churchman? |
| Feste | No such matter, sir. I do live by the church; for I do live at my house, and my house doth stand by the church. |
| Viola | So thou mayest say the king lies by a beggar, if a beggar dwell near him; or the church stands by thy tabor, if thy tabor stand by the church. 10 |
| Feste | You have said, sir. To see this age! A sentence is but a cheveril glove to a good wit—how quickly the wrong side may be turned outward! |
| Viola | Nay, that's certain; they that dally nicely with words may quickly make them wanton. |
| Feste | I would therefore my sister had had no name, sir. |
| Viola | Why, man? |
| Feste | Why, sir, her name's a word, and to dally with that word might make my sister wanton. But, indeed, words are very rascals since bonds disgraced them. 20 |
| Viola | Thy reason, man? |
| Feste | Troth, sir, I can yield you none without words, and words are grown so false I am loth to prove reason with them. |

26    **carest for:** 'worry about' and 'like'

28–29    **in my conscience:** to speak the truth

29–31    **If that . . . invisible:** *a flippant way of saying he has had enough of Cesario's company*

35    *It was a popular joke that wives made fools of their husbands.*
      **pilchards:** *small herrings*

37    **her corrupter of words:** *a title which he earns in this scene*

38    **late:** lately (*Viola had heard Feste sing to Orsino. She, too, is growing tired of this conversation, and has the idea of sending him to tell Olivia that she has returned.*)

39    **the orb:** our world

40    **but:** unless

43    **I think . . . there:** *Feste sarcastically calls Cesario a wise man.*
      **there:** at Olivia's house

44    **an thou pass upon me:** if you are starting to jibe at me

45    *Viola feels she can best get rid of Feste by paying him the tip,* 'expenses', *he would expect for his demonstration of wit.*

46–47    'Next time Jove comes around giving out beards and moustaches, I hope he won't forget you.' (*Feste jokingly comments on Cesario's youthful looks.*)

48–49    *Feste thinks this is merely agreeing with his last remark, but to the audience it recalls Viola's love-sickness for Orsino. Like any fashionable gentleman, Orsino wears a beard. Viola is really speaking more to herself, emphasising* 'my'.

51    *Feste thinks he is on to a good thing and tries to wheedle more money. He says that one coin looks very lonely by itself.*

52    **put to use:** loaned out on interest (*so money would* 'breed' *money*) or mated (*like animals on a farm*)

53–54    *During the war at Troy* (Phrygia), *Pandarus helped the young lovers Troilus and Cressida to come together. Feste sees himself, fancifully, as playing a similar role to bring together the coin in his hand with another from Cesario's purse. His efforts are successful—line 55.*

56    **The matter . . . great:** 'It's a mere trifle' (*According to the story, Cressida later became a leper, who would have to* 'beg' *for a living.*)

| | |
|---|---|
| Viola | I warrant thou art a merry fellow, and carest for nothing. |
| Feste | Not so, sir. I do care for something; but, in my conscience, sir, I do not care for you. If that be to care for nothing, sir, I would it would make you invisible. |
| Viola | Art not thou the Lady Olivia's fool? |
| Feste | No, indeed, sir, the Lady Olivia has no folly; she will keep no fool, sir, till she be married. And fools are as like husbands as pilchards are to herrings—the husband's the bigger. I am indeed not her fool, but her corrupter of words. |
| Viola | I saw thee late at the Count Orsino's. |
| Feste | Foolery, sir, does walk about the orb like the sun; it shines everywhere. I would be sorry, sir, but the fool should be as oft with your master as with my mistress. I think I saw your wisdom there. |
| Viola | Nay, an thou pass upon me, I'll no more with thee. Hold, there's expenses for thee. |
| Feste | Now, Jove, in his next commodity of hair, send thee a beard. |
| Viola | By my troth, I'll tell thee, I am almost sick for one; though I would not have it grow on mv chin. Is thy lady within? |
| Feste | Would not a pair of these have bred, sir? |
| Viola | Yes, being kept together and put to use. |
| Feste | I would play Lord Pandarus of Phrygia, sir, to bring a Cressida to this Troilus. |
| Viola | I understand you, sir; 'tis well begged. |
| Feste | The matter, I hope, is not great, sir—begging but a beggar; Cressida was a beggar. My lady is |

30

40

50

58    **construe:** explain

59–60    **out of my welkin:** beyond my knowledge

61    **overworn:** over-used (*Feste deliberately chooses an unusual word, 'welkin'—literally 'sky'—because he scorns to imitate the vocabulary of people who try to be fashionable.*)

62    *Viola is not so wrapped up in her own troubles that she cannot spare some sympathy for Feste's difficult job.*

62–70    'This man is clever enough to be a professional fool. To be a skilful fool you need some intelligence. To imitate someone, a jester must carefully take note of that person's mood and his rank in society, and must choose a time when people are ready to laugh; and like an untrained hawk he must fly off in pursuit of any bird he sees. (*The jester cannot afford to miss any possible material for a joke.*) It's as hard to be a good jester as to be a wise man, for his skill in revealing the folly in others is an important service, whereas wise men who lapse into folly only make complete idiots of themselves.' (*The rhyme makes this comparison sound like a proverb, full of wisdom. The play delights in showing how men make fools of themselves. Immediately Viola has spoken one such gentleman-fool enters with Sir Toby.*)

73    'God save you, sir.'

74    'And you too; I am at your service.' (*Sir Andrew's flourish in showing off his French before a servant falls flat when Viola replies easily in French. Lamely, he has to continue the conversation in English.*)

76–77    'Will you come in? It is my niece's wish, if your business is with her.' (*Sir Toby shows scorn for Cesario by deliberately using affected language: 'encounter', 'desirous', 'trade'.*)

78–79    'I am on my way to see your niece, or rather she is as far as I am going.' (*Viola continues the shipping metaphor suggested by Sir Toby's word 'trade'.*)

80    **Taste:** try out

81    **understand:** stand under (*Viola puns on the word and pretends not to know what Sir Toby means, to get her own back for his rudeness in using affected language.*)

85    **with gait and entrance:** 'by walking and going into the house' (*through the garden 'gate'—on which she is punning*)

86    **prevented:** anticipated (*Olivia's eagerness to see Cesario again makes her forget her dignity and go to meet him.*)

within, sir. I will construe to them whence you come; who you are and what you would are out of my welkin—I might say 'element', but the word is overworn.

*Exit*

| | |
|---|---|
| Viola | This fellow is wise enough to play the fool, |
| | And, to do that well, craves a kind of wit. |
| | He must observe their mood on whom he jests, |
| | The quality of persons, and the time; |
| | And, like the haggard, check at every feather |
| | That comes before his eye. This is a practice |
| | As full of labour as a wise man's art; |
| | For folly that he wisely shows is fit; |
| | But wise men, folly-fallen, quite taint their wit. 70 |

*Enter* Sir Toby *and* Sir Andrew

| | |
|---|---|
| Toby | Save you, gentleman. |
| Viola | And you, sir. |
| Andrew | Dieu vous garde, monsieur. |
| Viola | Et vous aussi; votre serviteur. |
| Andrew | I hope, sir, you are; and I am yours. |
| Toby | Will you encounter the house? My niece is desirous you should enter, if your trade be to her. |
| Viola | I am bound to your niece, sir. I mean, she is the list of my voyage. |
| Toby | Taste your legs, sir; put them to motion. 80 |
| Viola | My legs do better understand me, sir, than I understand what you mean by bidding me taste my legs. |
| Toby | I mean, to go, sir; to enter. |
| Viola | I will answer you with gait and entrance, but we are prevented. |

| | |
|---|---|
| 87 | *Viola greets Olivia in the same high-flown courtier's language as she used before to deliver Orsino's message. Sir Andrew, who considers Orsino his rival for Olivia, can only listen in amazement and write down this useful vocabulary in his notebook (line 93).* |
| 91–92 | 'What I have to say to you must be said in private.' |
| 92 | **pregnant:** receptive |
| | **vouchsafed:** condescending to listen |
| 95–96 | **my hearing:** 'what I have to hear from Orsino' |
| 97 | *Olivia takes the chance to lean upon Cesario's arm. She doesn't even trouble to ask what is Orsino's message.* |
| 101 | **servant:** *This word was often used to mean 'a lover'. Olivia is disappointed that Cesario uses it in only its ordinary sense. If Cesario wants to be an ordinary servant, let him stay in Orsino's service (line 103).* |
| 101–102 | **'Twas ... compliment:** 'The world's a miserable place now that a man is considered polite when he goes around pretending he enjoys being humble.' |
| 104 | **his:** the servants Orsino owns |
| 104–105 | *Viola is certainly saying that Orsino wishes to be Olivia's lover, but leaves it vague whether she herself will be still a servant or a lover. She cannot yet openly offend Olivia, so she tries to turn the conversation away from herself.* |
| 106–108 | 'As for him, I don't think about him. I would prefer him to have an empty mind rather than he should think about me.' |
| 109 | **whet:** sharpen *(Viola is still obeying her master's instructions and suggesting that just as a blunt knife can be sharpened, so can Olivia's apparently dull feelings for Orsino.)* |
| 111–115 | 'If I may interrupt you—I told you never to speak about him again, but if you chose instead to tell me about somebody else's love for me *(Viola cannot pretend to misunderstand Olivia this time)*, then I should find it the sweetest thing in the world to hear you beg me to love that person.' |
| 115 | **music from the spheres:** *According to the Greeks, the rotation of the planets fixed on their crystal spheres produced a marvellous harmony which men, unfortunately, could not hear.* |

*Enter* Olivia *and* Maria

Most excellent accomplished lady, the heavens rain odours on you!

Andrew    That youth's a rare courtier! 'Rain odours!' Well!                                              90

Viola     My matter hath no voice, lady, but to your own most pregnant and vouchsafed ear.

Andrew    'Odours', 'pregnant' and 'vouchsafed'; I'll get them all three all ready.

Olivia    Let the garden door be shut, and leave me to my hearing.

*Exeunt* Sir Toby, Sir Andrew *and* Maria

Give me your hand, sir.

Viola     My duty, madam, and most humble service.

Olivia    What is your name?

Viola     Cesario is your servant's name, fair princess.    100

Olivia    My 'servant', sir? 'Twas never merry world
          Since lowly feigning was called compliment.
          You're 'servant' to the Count Orsino, youth.

Viola     And he is yours, and his must needs be yours;
          Your servant's servant is your servant, madam.

Olivia    For him, I think not on him; for his thoughts,
          Would they were blanks, rather than filled with me!

Viola     Madam, I come to whet your gentle thoughts
          On his behalf.                                                                    110

Olivia    O, by your leave, I pray you;
          I bade you never speak again of him.
          But would you undertake another suit,
          I had rather hear you to solicit that
          Than music from the spheres.

117–124     'Let me speak, please. After the spell you put upon me at your last visit, I sent a ring after you; by doing so, I deceived myself, my servant Malvolio, and, I'm afraid, you also. You must have judged my behaviour very harshly; there I was thrusting on to you in such a shameful and underhand way something which you knew very well didn't belong to you. What were you likely to make of it?' (*Olivia realises that, as Cesario will not take the hint to speak, she must openly declare her love. Yet she is ashamed of herself. Her very awkwardness makes the audience sympathise; she has ceased to be the proud grand lady.*)

125     *Olivia compares her painful situation to that of a bear fastened to a* 'stake' *and attacked,* 'baited', *by savage,* 'unmuzzled', *dogs.*

126–127     **the unmuzzled ... think:** 'the worst mental torture a cruel tyrant could dream up'

128–130     **To one ... speak:** 'I have explained things clearly enough for someone as perceptive as you are. My feelings must be obvious to you. Now, what have you to say?'

129     **a cypress:** a transparent veil Olivia would wear as mourning

132     'Pity can be the first stage towards love.'

133–134     'Not one step, for it is a common enough experience to feel pity for one's enemies.'

135     'Let's forget about it then.' (*Olivia tries hard to treat Cesario's rejection of her offered love as though it meant little to her, but her annoyance at both Cesario and herself keeps breaking through.*)

136     *Olivia thinks that the only reason Cesario scorns her is that Cesario, being a poor man, is too proud to think of loving a lady so much his superior.*

137–138     *She would prefer to have Orsino her enemy, for at least he behaves nobly like the lion, than Cesario, who is more like the subtle and cruel wolf because he refuses her his love.*

139     *Olivia has almost got control of herself again and tells Cesario that the interview is over. Yet she envies the lucky woman who eventually will marry Cesario.*

141–142     'When you have ripened in age and wisdom (*and are therefore ready for marriage*) your wife will find herself with a fine, ('proper'), husband.'

143     **due west:** *Cesario is like the sun sinking out of Olivia's life.*

144     *Viola jauntily ignores Olivia's melancholy farewell and replies with the common cry of Thames watermen announcing their route up the river.*

145–147     *A very formal farewell, wishing Olivia health and peace of mind*

| | |
|---|---|
| Viola | Dear lady— |
| Olivia | Give me leave, beseech you. I did send, |
| | After the last enchantment you did here, |
| | A ring in chase of you. So did I abuse |
| | Myself, my servant and, I fear me, you. 120 |
| | Under your hard construction must I sit, |
| | To force that on you in a shameful cunning |
| | Which you knew none of yours. What might |
| | you think? |
| | Have you not set mine honour at the stake, |
| | And baited it with all the unmuzzled thoughts |
| | That tyrannous heart can think? |
| | To one of your receiving |
| | Enough is shown; a cypress, not a bosom, |
| | Hides my heart; so let me hear you speak. 130 |
| Viola | I pity you. |
| Olivia | That's a degree to love. |
| Viola | No, not a grize; for 'tis a vulgar proof |
| | That very oft we pity enemies. |
| Olivia | Why then, methinks 'tis time to smile again. |
| | O world, how apt the poor are to be proud! |
| | If one should be a prey, how much the better |
| | To fall before the lion than the wolf! |

*Clock strikes*

| | |
|---|---|
| | The clock upbraids me with the waste of time. |
| | Be not afraid, good youth, I will not have you, 140 |
| | And yet, when wit and youth is come to harvest, |
| | Your wife is like to reap a proper man. |
| | There lies your way, due west. |
| Viola | Then westward-ho! |
| | Grace and good disposition attend your |
| | ladyship! |

*and reminding her that Cesario was supposed to be there on Orsino'*
*behalf. Olivia, however, cannot let it all end like that and calls aft*
*the departing messenger.*

149    *Both girls are on edge and spar with words. Their riddle-like comm*
*ments mean more to the audience than to each other. It is as thoug*
*they are reluctant to tell each other too much of the truth.*

150    *Viola means that Olivia is wrong in thinking herself in love with*
*man. Olivia thinks she is being reminded that she is acting in a wa*
*beneath the dignity of a noble lady.*

151    'Then aren't you also forgetting your position?'

152    *As with Orsino, Viola can come within a fraction of revealing th*
*truth, and yet leave Olivia completely baffled.*

155    *Wistfully, Viola considers anything would be better than her presen*
*ridiculous position.*

156    *There is often something most attractive about a person in anger o*
*full of scorn. Viola's outburst finally makes Olivia throw aside al*
*restraint and speak her love. The scene ends with 18 lines of rhymin*
*couplets. Both Olivia and Viola are very worked up and use thi*
*artificial method of speaking as a way of putting some restrain*
*on their feelings, just as a poet often finds it a help to use a stri*
*verse form.*

158–169    'Love which you try to keep hidden reveals itself just a*
quickly as the guilt which causes the murderer to give himsel*
away; while a lover thinks no one knows of his feelings, they*
are only too obvious to everyone. Cesario, I swear by every*
thing I hold sacred, that, in spite of your pride, my love is s*
overwhelming that neither commonsense nor caution can*
silence it. Don't argue from this that, just because the woman*
in this case has done the wooing, you, the man, should no*
respond; instead, convince yourself by arguing that, whereas*
it is very satisfying to win a person's love, it is even more*
agreeable to be made a present of love.'

175    **deplore:** tell sadly

177    **his:** *Olivia refers to Orsino, but perhaps she is also thinking there*
*may still be a chance that Cesario's heart may change.*

|  | You'll nothing, madam, to my lord by me? |
| Olivia | Stay. |
|  | I prithee, tell me what thou thinkest of me? |
| Viola | That you do think you are not what you are. 150 |
| Olivia | If I think so, I think the same of you. |
| Viola | Then think you right; I am not what I am. |
| Olivia | I would you were as I would have you be. |
| Viola | Would it be better, madam, than I am? |
|  | I wish it might, for now I am your fool. |
| Olivia | O, what a deal of scorn looks beautiful |
|  | In the contempt and anger of his lip! |
|  | A murderous guilt shows not itself more soon |
|  | Than love that would seem hid. Love's night is noon. 160 |
|  | Cesario, by the roses of the spring, |
|  | By maidhood, honour, truth and everything, |
|  | I love thee so, that, maugre all thy pride, |
|  | Nor wit nor reason can my passion hide. |
|  | Do not extort thy reasons from this clause, |
|  | For that I woo, thou therefore hast no cause; |
|  | But rather reason thus with reason fetter: |
|  | Love sought is good, but given unsought is better. |
| Viola | By innocence I swear, and by my youth, 170 |
|  | I have one heart, one bosom and one truth, |
|  | And that no woman has, nor never none |
|  | Shall mistress be of it, save I alone. |
|  | And so adieu, good madam! Never more |
|  | Will I my master's tears to you deplore. |
| Olivia | Yet come again; for thou perhaps mayest move |
|  | That heart which now abhors to like his love. |

*Exeunt*

A fresh difficulty is about to face Viola. Not content with his plot against Malvolio, Sir Toby is also planning to make a fool of his so-called 'friend', Sir Andrew, by involving him in a comical duel with Orsino's messenger. It will serve to make Sir Andrew forget his hopeless quest for Olivia and his genuine threat to go home, which would leave Sir Toby without his source of money.

6     **orchard:** *Olivia's garden where the last scene was set.*

9     **argument:** proof

11     'Do you expect me to believe that?'

12–13     **oaths of judgment and reason:** *When a legal oath was taken one referred to truth, judgment and reason. By omitting the first, Fabian prepares the audience, but not Sir Andrew, for a highly imaginary explanation.*

14–15     'Since the time of the Flood, proof has always been established by using judgment and reason.'

16–28     *Sir Andrew lets himself be convinced not by logic but by sheer weight of words. Fabian's speech becomes more and more preposterous and his metaphors tumble over each other. A less colourful version would be:*
'She went out of her way to show interest in Cesario knowing you were watching, in order to provoke you, to awaken your spirit of daring, to incense you and fill you with burning rage. You should have gone up to her, and with some dazzling remark just that minute made up left Cesario speechless with amazement. She expected this, and you let the chance slip. You missed this golden opportunity, and now you must hold the coldest place in Olivia's affection, where you are likely to remain unless you can regain her admiration by some daring or ingenious deed.'

17–18     **dormouse valour:** 'Dormouse' *may be Fabian's deliberate mistake for 'dormant', but it applies very aptly to Sir Andrew, who, like the dormouse, is one of the most timorous of creatures.*

23–24     **double gilt . . . wash off:** *The best quality gilt plating was twice washed in gold; so this chance was doubly valuable because Sir Andrew could have shown both how much he loved Olivia and how much cleverer he was than Cesario.*

26–27     **like an icicle . . . beard:** *The icicle is suggested by the* 'sailing into the north' *metaphor, and the Dutchman was one of the Dutch explorers of the Arctic whose tales had caught the popular imagination.*

SCENE 2  Olivia's house

*Enter* Sir Toby, Sir Andrew *and* Fabian.

Andrew    No, faith, I'll not stay a jot longer.

Toby      Thy reason, dear venom, give thy reason.

Fabian    You must needs yield your reason, Sir Andrew.

Andrew    Marry, I saw your niece do more favours to the
          count's serving-man than ever she bestowed upon
          me; I saw it in the orchard.

Toby      Did she see thee the while, old boy? Tell me that.

Andrew    As plain as I see you now.

Fabian    This was a great argument of love in her toward
          you.                                                    10

Andrew    'Slight, will you make an ass of me?

Fabian    I will prove it legitimate, sir, upon the oaths of
          judgment and reason.

Toby      And they have been grand-jurymen since before
          Noah was a sailor.

Fabian    She did show favour to the youth in your sight,
          only to exasperate you, to awake your dormouse
          valour, to put fire in your heart and brimstone in
          your liver. You should then have accosted her
          and, with some excellent jests, fire-new from the      20
          mint, you should have banged the youth into
          dumbness. This was looked for at your hand, and
          this was balked; the double gilt of this oppor-
          tunity you let time wash off, and you are now
          sailed into the north of my lady's opinion, where
          you will hang like an icicle on a Dutchman's
          beard, unless you do redeem it by some laudable
          attempt either of valour or policy.

| | |
|---|---|
| 30–31 | **policy, politician:** *To many Elizabethans, as to Sir Andrew, these were scornful words, suggesting underhand intrigue.* |
| 30 | **I had as lief be:** I would just as soon be |
| | **a Brownist:** *a follower of Robert Brown's extremist Puritan sect, and so intensely unpopular with the theatre-going public* |
| 34 | **eleven:** *Fabian's exaggeration has affected Sir Toby too.* |
| 35–38 | **there is ... valour:** 'there is nothing like a man's reputation for bravery to make a woman think well of him.' |
| 36 | **love-broker:** one who arranges love affairs |
| 41–45 | 'Write it in a style fit for a fighting man. Be bitter and to the point. There's no need for your letter to make sense, provided that it reads well and is full of original flourishes (*like Fabian's last long speech*). Taunt him as you are free to do in a letter. It won't be out of place if you refer to him in an offensively familiar way.' (*To refer to anyone but a close friend as 'thou' instead of 'you', would be considered too familiar and in this case a deliberate insult.*) |
| 47 | **the bed of Ware:** *Thinking first of sheets of paper, then of bed-sheets, reminds Sir Toby of the biggest bed he and the audience have heard of—that at the inn at Ware which could hold about 12 people.* |
| 48 | **gall:** bitterness (*and a pun on 'oak-gall' used in the making of ink*) |
| 49 | **goose-pen:** *Pens were made from the quills of a goose, the supposedly cowardly bird—another jibe at Sir Andrew.* |
| 52 | **cubiculo:** *Sir Toby shows off with an Italian word for the room in which Sir Andrew would be writing the challenge.* |
| 53 | **manakin:** puppet (*Sir Toby manipulates Sir Andrew as easily as though he controlled him by strings.*) |
| 54 | **dear:** expensive (*Sir Toby puns on the word and again reminds the audience of his only interest in Sir Andrew.*) |
| 55 | **strong:** at the very least |
| 58–59 | 'If I do deliver it, then never rely on me again. We must now do all we can to provoke Cesario into accepting the challenge.' |
| 59 | **wainropes:** cart-ropes |

| | |
|---|---|
| Andrew | An it be any way, it must be with valour, for policy I hate; I had as lief be a Brownist as a politician. 30 |
| Toby | Why then, build me thy fortunes upon the basis of valour. Challenge me the count's youth to fight with him, hurt him in eleven places; my niece shall take note of it; and, assure thyself, there is no love-broker in the world can more prevail in man's commendation with woman than report of valour. |
| Fabian | There is no way but this, Sir Andrew. |
| Andrew | Will either of you bear me a challenge to him? 40 |
| Toby | Go, write it in a martial hand; be curst and brief. It is no matter how witty, so it be eloquent and full of invention; taunt him with the licence of ink; if thou 'thou'st' him some thrice, it shall not be amiss; and as many lies as will lie in thy sheet of paper—although the sheet were big enough for the bed of Ware in England—set them down; go, about it. Let there be gall enough in thy ink, though thou write with a goose-pen, no matter; about it. 50 |
| Andrew | Where shall I find you? |
| Toby | We'll call thee at the cubiculo. Go! |

*Exit* Sir Andrew

| | |
|---|---|
| Fabian | This is a dear manakin to you, Sir Toby. |
| Toby | I have been dear to him, lad, some two thousand strong or so. |
| Fabian | We shall have a rare letter from him; but you'll not deliver it? |
| Toby | Never trust me then. And by all means stir on the youth to an answer. I think oxen and wain- |

| | |
|---|---|
| 60 | **hale:** drag (*Sir Toby is not pushing Sir Andrew into a serious quarrel, for he has rightly judged that Cesario is no fighter.*) |
| 61–62 | **blood in his liver:** *A coward was supposed to have very little blood in his liver.* |
| 63 | **anatomy:** body (*Sir Toby considers Sir Andrew little more than a walking corpse.*) |
| 64–65 | 'And there's not much to suggest cruelty in the face of his opponent, the young man.' |
| 66 | **youngest wren of nine:** 'the last (and therefore smallest) member of a large family of wrens' (*The* 'wren' *is another reference to Maria's dwarf stature as she comes in bubbling over with laughter.*) |
| 67 | **spleen:** fit of laughter |
| 69 | **renegado:** deserter from the true faith (*Maria says that no one in his right senses could possibly have believed the letter she contrived for Malvolio to find, and yet Malvolio has believed it because he has followed all the instructions.*) |
| 71–72 | **impossible . . . grossness:** incredibly stupid behaviour |
| 74–75 | **pedant . . . church:** *Schoolmasters were often figures of fun and might still be wearing the old-fashioned cross-gartering. Village children were often taught in a little room over the church porch.* |
| 78–79 | **new map . . . Indies:** *Malvolio's face creased with smiling reminds Maria of a recently published map of the world, drawn in 1600, and bearing a criss-cross pattern of navigational lines. It included the East* 'Indies'. |
| 79 | **augmentation:** latest detail |
| 80–81 | **hurling things . . . strike:** *It was not an age to show much sympathy towards lunatics.* |

|              | ropes cannot hale them together. For Andrew, if   60 |
|              | he were opened, and you find so much blood in |
|              | his liver as will clog the foot of a flea, I'll eat the |
|              | rest of the anatomy. |

Fabian      And his opposite, the youth, bears in his visage
            no great presage of cruelty.

            *Enter* Maria

Toby        Look, where the youngest wren of nine comes!

Maria       If you desire the spleen, and will laugh yourselves
            into stitches, follow me. Yond gull, Malvolio, is
            turned heathen—a very renegado; for there is no
            Christian that means to be saved by believing    70
            rightly can ever believe such impossible passages
            of grossness. He's in yellow stockings!

Toby        And cross-gartered?

Maria       Most villainously—like a pedant that keeps a
            school in the church. I have dogged him like his
            murderer. He does obey every point of the letter
            that I dropped to betray him; he does smile his
            face into more lines than is in the new map with
            the augmentation of the Indies. You have not
            seen such a thing as it is. I can hardly forbear hur-   80
            ling things at him; I know my lady will strike
            him; if she do, he'll smile and take it for a great
            favour.

Toby        Come, bring us, bring us where he is.

                                                    *Exeunt*

Just as a film will show two separate actions happening simultaneously, by cutting from one to the other as the two sets of characters move nearer and nearer to their inevitable meeting, so Shakespeare keeps reminding the audience of Sebastian's approach. Antonio has caught up with his friend just before they enter, and Sebastian has been protesting at Antonio's putting himself out just for him.

1  **troubled you:** 'inconvenienced you by asking you to come with me'

2  'since you enjoy taking trouble for me'

4  *Antonio speaks impulsively and a little breathlessly after hurrying after Sebastian, so his sentences are broken ones. He says he has been driven by the sharpest impulse, as a horse is driven by spurs.*

6–13  'It wasn't just that I wanted to see you again—though I admit I was so eager to see you again that I would have followed you much further, if necessary—but I was anxious about what might happen to you as you wandered about with no experience of this country. It is a country which often turns out to be unfriendly to a man who has to find his way through it without help. I was ready enough to come, but it was these reasons I had for fearing for your safety that, in fact, made me set out after you.'

16–19  'Good turns are often idly dismissed with some such worthless reward (*his words of thanks, he means, are of no value to Antonio*). But if I were as certain of being wealthy as I am certain that I am in your debt, you would be better rewarded.'

21  **relics:** ancient remains (*Sebastian has a young man's eagerness to make the most of his situation. He is in a new country and is keen to act like any tourist. Antonio is both older and more cautious. Their separation, so naturally arranged, is necessary for the plot.*)

26  **renown:** make famous

29  **Count his:** Count's

SCENE 3   A street
*Enter* Sebastian *and* Antonio.

Sebas.  I would not by my will have troubled you,
But, since you make your pleasure of your pains,
I will no further chide you.

Antonio  I could not stay behind you; my desire,
More sharp than filed steel, did spur me forth;
And not all love to see you—though so much
As might have drawn one to a longer voyage—
But jealousy what might befall your travel,
Being skilless in these parts; which to a stranger,
Unguided and unfriended, often prove                    10
Rough and unhospitable. My willing love,
The rather by these arguments of fear,
Set forth in your pursuit.

Sebas.  My kind Antonio,
I can no other answer make but thanks
And thanks; and ever oft good turns
Are shuffled off with such uncurrent pay.
But were my worth as is my conscience firm,
You should find better dealing.
   What's to do?                                        20
Shall we go see the relics of this town?

Antonio  Tomorrow, sir; best first go see your lodging.

Sebas.  I am not weary, and 'tis long to night.
I pray you, let us satisfy our eyes
With the memorials and the things of fame
That do renown this city.

Antonio  Would you'd pardon me;
I do not without danger walk these streets.
Once, in a sea-fight against the Count his galleys,

| | |
|---|---|
| 30–32 | *Antonio is modest, and Sebastian has to draw the full account out of him. Details are never just background information in Shakespeare and this piece of Antonio's history will have its effect on the story later.* |

**of such . . . answered:** 'which became so well-known that if I were captured, it would be next to impossible to atone for the offence' (*except by Antonio's death*)

33     **Belike:** I suppose

34–42    'It wasn't as bad as that, although the conditions at that time and the sort of quarrel it was might easily have led to bloodshed. The whole thing could have been settled afterwards by restoring what we had seized from them, and that is what most men in our city did so that they could resume trading (*with Illyria*). I was the only one who refused to return the cargo. So that's the reason that I'll have a hard time of it if I'm caught here.'

44     **It doth not fit me:** I had better not

45     **the Elephant:** an inn

46     **bespeak our diet:** order our meal

50     **There shall you have me:** You will find me there (*at the inn*)

51     'Why should I need your purse?'

52–54    'Perhaps you will see some trifling thing you would like to buy, and you haven't yourself enough money to throw away on luxuries.'

|          | I did some service, of such note indeed | 30 |
|          | That were I taken here it would scarce be answered. | |

Sebas.    Belike you slew great number of his people?

Antonio    The offence is not of such a bloody nature,
Albeit the quality of the time and quarrel
Might well have given us bloody argument.
It might have since been answered in repaying
What we took from them, which, for traffic's sake,
Most of our city did; only myself stood out,    40
For which, if I be lapsed in this place,
I shall pay dear.

Sebas.    Do not then walk too open.

Antonio    It doth not fit me. Hold, sir, here's my purse.
In the south suburbs at the Elephant
Is best to lodge. I will bespeak our diet,
Whiles you beguile the time and feed your knowledge
With viewing of the town.
There shall you have me.    50

Sebas.    Why I your purse?

Antonio    Haply your eye shall light upon some toy
You have desire to purchase; and your store,
I think, is not for idle markets, sir.

Sebas.    I'll be your purse-bearer, and leave you
For an hour.

Antonio    To the Elephant.

Sebas.    I do remember.

*Exeunt*

This is Sir Toby's big moment. He gets even with Malvolio, proves Sir Andrew an utter coward, and embarrasses Viola so much that she is just about to disclose her identity when Antonio arrives. Antonio's accidental appearance is the turning-point of the play. All the stories are brought together at one moment and only the unravelling remains to be done.

It is no surprise to the audience that Olivia has not been able to put Cesario out of her mind. The messenger she has sent to persuade Cesario to come again has not yet returned; meanwhile she is talking to herself in an agitated way.

1–8   'I have sent someone to fetch him and now he's on his way here. How shall I entertain him? What can I give him? It is easier to buy a young man than to beg or borrow from one. (*Olivia still believes she will be able to buy the love she wants, as though Cesario is up for sale.*) I must be careful—someone may hear me. Where's Malvolio? He's grave and dignified. In my present mood I could well do with so serious a servant.' (*There clearly couldn't be a worse moment for Malvolio to adopt his fantastic behaviour.*)

10   **possessed:** *Lunatics were thought to be possessed by devils.*

14   **tainted in his wits:** out of his mind

15–17   *Olivia is sadly sympathetic with Malvolio. She has no superior person's scorn for madness, because she realises only too well that her own behaviour is equally irresponsible—'merry madness'—in the eyes of the world.*

18   *Malvolio's splashes of vivid colour, his fawning smiles and his simpering familiarity make him a preposterous figure. Olivia is too amazed to laugh, but Maria chuckling in the background makes sure none of the comedy is missed by the audience.*

19   **upon a sad occasion:** on serious business

21   **obstruction in the blood:** *His garters are so tight that his blood is not freely circulating—so he might really feel unwell, 'sad'.*

22   **one:** *Olivia (said with a sly wink)*

22–23   **If it . . . sonnet is:** 'If you like to see me like this, then I agree with the words of the popular song'

27   **Not . . . mind:** 'I am not depressed' (*Black was associated with moods of melancholy.*)

SCENE 4    Olivia's garden

*Enter* Olivia *and* Maria.

Olivia    I have sent after him; he says he'll come.
How shall I feast him? What bestow of him?
For youth is bought more oft than begged or
borrowed.
I speak too loud.
    Where's Malvolio? He is sad and civil,
And suits well for a servant with my fortunes.
Where is Malvolio?

Maria    He's coming, madam; but in very strange manner.
He is sure possessed, madam.                              10

Olivia    Why, what's the matter? Does he rave?

Maria    No, madam, he does nothing but smile. Your
ladyship were best to have some guard about you
if he come, for sure the man is tainted in his wits.

Olivia    Go, call him hither. *(aside)* I am as mad as he,
If sad and merry madness equal be.

    *Enter* Malvolio

    How now, Malvolio?

Malv.    Sweet lady, ho, ho!

Olivia    Smilest thou? I sent for thee upon a sad occasion.

Malv.    Sad, lady? I could be sad; this does make some    20
obstruction in the blood, this cross-gartering; but
what of that? If it please the eye of one, it is with
me as the very true sonnet is: 'Please one, and
please all.'

Maria    Why, how dost thou, man? What is the matter
with thee?

Malv.    Not black in my mind, though yellow in my legs.

28–29    **It, his, we:** *Malvolio confidently implies that Olivia knows very well their little secret.*

29–30    **sweet Roman hand:** the new Italian style of handwriting, which a lady like Olivia would use

31    *Olivia's innocent suggestion that Malvolio should rest because he is ill is misinterpreted by the cocksure servant.*

35    'Have you gone out of your mind, Malvolio?'

36    'Do I have to answer you (*a mere servant*)? Though I suppose I must, just as sweet nightingales sing in response to wretched jackdaws.'

39–53    *Malvolio is so convinced that he is right that he lingers lovingly over the phrases of Olivia's supposed letter which he has learned by heart, while he quite ignores Olivia's obvious bewilderment. He is answering Maria's question but, in effect, he is talking for his own enjoyment.*

54    **very:** absolutely

     **midsummer madness:** *People thought that madness could be due to intense heat.*

|         | It did come to his hands, and commands shall be executed. I think we do know the sweet Roman hand. | 30 |
| --- | --- | --- |
| Olivia | Wilt thou go to bed, Malvolio? | |
| Malv. | To bed? Ay, sweetheart, and I'll come to thee. | |
| Olivia | God comfort thee! Why dost thou smile so, and kiss thy hand so oft? | |
| Maria | How do you, Malvolio? | |
| Malv. | At your request! Yes, nightingales answer daws. | |
| Maria | Why appear you with this ridiculous boldness before my lady? | |
| Malv. | '*Be not afraid of greatness*'—'twas well writ. | |
| Olivia | What meanest thou by that, Malvolio? | 40 |
| Malv. | '*Some are born great*'— | |
| Olivia | Ha? | |
| Malv. | '*Some achieve greatness*'— | |
| Olivia | What sayest thou? | |
| Malv. | '*And some have greatness thrust upon them.*' | |
| Olivia | Heaven restore thee! | |
| Malv. | '*Remember who commended thy yellow stockings*'— | |
| Olivia | Thy yellow stockings? | |
| Malv. | '*And wished to see thee cross-gartered.*' | |
| Olivia | Cross-gartered? | 50 |
| Malv. | '*Go to! Thou art made if thou desirest to be so.*' | |
| Olivia | Am I made? | |
| Malv. | '*If not, let me see thee a servant still.*' | |
| Olivia | Why, this is very midsummer madness! | |

*Enter* Servant

| Servant | Madam, the young gentleman of the Count Orsino's is returned. I could hardly entreat him |
| --- | --- |

58    *Olivia cannot spend any further time finding out what Malvolio is talking about. Cesario must have all her attention. She sends her uncle to act as her deputy, as the man about the house, while she is occupied elsewhere.*

59    **looked to:** looked after

61    **miscarry:** come to any harm

62    **dowry:** fortune

63    **come near:** begin to understand (*Malvolio thinks that Olivia was pretending not to understand him in order to deceive Maria; but he is now sure that in her last remarks she has given herself away.*)

70    **consequently:** afterwards, in the letter

71–73    **as a sad ... note:** 'a serious expression, a dignified posture, a way of talking as though every word was precious, like some highly respected gentleman' (*This is Malvolio's interpretation of how Olivia expects him to behave before Sir Toby. When Sir Toby and Fabian enter, it is as though Malvolio becomes a completely different character. His grotesque familiarity with Olivia gives way to a haughty stance and an exaggerated sneering tone.*)

73    **limed:** caught (*Birds were trapped by sticky bird-lime smeared on branches. Malvolio's speech is a comical mixture of pompous and crude ideas.*)

74, 82    **Jove:** *As when he found the letter, Malvolio smugly disclaims credit for catching Olivia, by pretending to be humbly passing on to the gods the praise he really feels is due to himself.*

76    **Fellow:** companion (*as Malvolio, but not Olivia, understands the word to mean*)

76–77    **after my degree:** in a way appropriate to my status (*as a steward*)

77–80    **everything ... said:** 'everything fits together, so that not the least scrap of an objection, not the smallest scrap of a scrap, nothing at all, however incredible or uncertain—need I say more?' ('Drams' *and* 'scruples'—*on which he is punning—were both small weights. He is delighted by his skill in thinking of such a variety of words for saying the same thing. He pauses in mid-sentence lost in self-admiration.*)

84–86    'Where is he, by all that's holy? Even if all the devils in hell are squeezed into his one body, and the whole flock of devils ('Legion himself') in control of him, yet I'll speak to him.' (*Sir Toby and his friends creep up warily pretending to be scared of the devil that has possessed Malvolio, and that they are very daring to speak to him.*)

|  |  |
|---|---|
|  | back; he attends your ladyship's pleasure. |
| Olivia | I'll come to him. (*Exit* Servant) Good Maria, let this fellow be looked to. Where's my cousin Toby? Let some of my people have a special care of him; 60 I would not have him miscarry for the half of my dowry. |

*Exeunt* Olivia *and* Maria

| Malv. | O ho! Do you come near me now? No worse man than Sir Toby to look to me! This concurs directly with the letter; she sends him on purpose, that I may appear stubborn to him; for she incites me to that in the letter. '*Cast thy humble slough,*' says she; '*be opposite with a kinsman, surly with servants; let thy tongue tang with arguments of state; put thyself into the trick of singularity*'; and consequently sets 70 down the manner how: as a sad face, a reverend carriage, a slow tongue, in the habit of some sir of note, and so forth. I have limed her; but it is Jove's doing, and Jove make me thankful! And when she went away now, 'Let this fellow be looked to'. 'Fellow!' Not 'Malvolio', nor after my degree, but 'fellow'. Why, everything adheres together, that no dram of a scruple, no scruple of a scruple, no obstacle, no incredulous or unsafe circumstance—what can be said?—nothing that 80 can be can come between me and the full prospect of my hopes. Well, Jove, not I, is the doer of this, and he is to be thanked! |
|---|---|

*Enter* Sir Toby, Fabian *and* Maria

| Toby | Which way is he, in the name of sanctity? If all the devils of hell be drawn in little, and Legion himself possessed him, yet I'll speak to him. |
|---|---|

| | |
|---|---|
| 89–90 | 'Get away, I have nothing to do with you; let me enjoy my privacy.' (*Malvolio too is enjoying himself in this role, but he little knows that he is acting exactly as Maria and Sir Toby planned.*) |
| 91 | **hollow:** *as though the devil were deep-down inside him* |
| 94 | *This seems to confirm Malvolio's opinion.* |
| 95 | **Go to:** Be careful |
| 96 | **let me alone:** leave it to me |
| | **How do you, Malvolio?:** *Sir Toby oozes sympathy.* |
| 97 | **defy the devil:** don't give in to the devil so easily |
| 99 | *Things are not going quite as Malvolio expected. Sir Toby's tone annoys him.* |
| 100 | **La, you:** Just listen to that |
| 102 | *A primitive urine-test, made by a sort of kindly witch—the* 'wise woman'—*could be used to diagnose diseases.* |
| 104–105 | **My lady . . . say:** *These are the words Malvolio would have longed to hear, but following Fabian's coarseness they only increase his fury.* |
| 109 | **move:** make him worse |
| 113 | *Sir Toby adopts a new insultingly colloquial manner, treating Malvolio as a naughty child.* |
| | **bawcock:** fine fellow (*a contemptuous expression*) |
| 114 | **chuck:** my old cock sparrow |
| 116 | **Biddy:** *the name by which children would call in chickens— suggested by* 'cock' *and* 'chuck' |
| 116–118 | **'Tis not . . . collier:** 'A serious person like yourself mustn't play games with the devil; leave him to his own devices.' |
| 117 | **cherry-pit:** a children's game of throwing cherry-stones into a hole |

| | |
|---|---|
| Fabian | Here he is, here he is. How is it with you, sir? How is it with you, man? |
| Malv. | Go off, I discard you; let me enjoy my private; go off. 90 |
| Maria | Lo, how hollow the fiend speaks within him! Did not I tell you? Sir Toby, my lady prays you to have a care of him. |
| Malv. | Ah ha! Does she so? |
| Toby | Go to, go to! Peace, peace! We must deal gently with him; let me alone. How do you, Malvolio? How is it with you? What, man, defy the devil! Consider, he's an enemy to mankind. |
| Malv. | Do you know what you say? |
| Maria | La, you, an you speak ill of the devil, how he 100 takes it at heart! Pray God he be not bewitched! |
| Fabian | Carry his water to the wise woman. |
| Maria | Marry, and it shall be done tomorrow morning if I live. My lady would not lose him for more than I'll say. |
| Malv. | How now, mistress! |
| Maria | O Lord! |
| Toby | Prithee, hold thy peace! This is not the way. Do you not see you move him? Let me alone with him. 110 |
| Fabian | No way but gentleness; gently, gently! The fiend is rough, and will not be roughly used. |
| Toby | Why, how now, my bawcock? How dost thou, chuck? |
| Malv. | Sir! |
| Toby | Ay, Biddy, come with me. What, man! 'Tis not for gravity to play at cherry-pit with Satan. Hang |

118     **foul collier:** *The devil was thought to be grimy like a coal-miner from the blackest regions of hell.*

119     *Prayer might turn his mind from association with the devil.*

121     **minx:** *Malvolio spits out his rage at Maria, which she accepts tolerantly, pretending it is a further sign that the devil is inside him.*

124     **I am . . . element:** 'I don't belong in your world'

124–125     *Malvolio's empty threat is answered only by delighted laughter. Sir Toby and Fabian cannot believe their plot could have worked so well.*

129–130     'This trick has got hold of him like a disease.'

129     **genius:** basic nature (*Malvolio has been caught because the plot played on his vanity.*)

131–132     *Again it is Maria who keeps the plot moving; she wants to play it out to the end.*

    **lest . . . taint:** 'in case the plot becomes known and so is ruined' (*A wound was believed to become worse if exposed to the air.*)

133     *Fabian thinks they might be carrying it too far, but Maria has no such qualms.*

134     **quieter:** *because Malvolio will not be around to scold them*

135     *This was normal treatment for lunatics.*

137     **carry it thus:** 'keep up the trick until we've reached that stage' (*Sir Toby reassures the audience that it will all end as a joke. He has no intention of really driving Malvolio mad; that would spoil the mood of the comedy.*)

138     **till . . . breath:** 'until the joke has worn itself out'

140     **bring . . . bar:** 'reveal the plot for everyone to admire'

140, 141     **bar, crown, finder:** *Sir Toby puns on the idea of Maria acting as coroner, 'crowner', in the law court, 'at the bar', and bringing in the judgment, 'finding', of madness on Malvolio.*

142     'Here's more fun on its way!' (*May 1st was a day of revels.*)

143–144     **there's . . . in it:** 'it's full of bite' (*Sir Andrew is delighted with his composition. He prides himself on his quarrelling technique—the art of provoking your opponent to make the actual challenge. He dances round Sir Toby and Fabian missing the mockery in their praise.*)

146     **I warrant him:** 'I'm sure he (*Cesario*) will find it so'

|          | him, foul collier! |
| Maria | Get him to say his prayers, good Sir Toby; get him to pray. 120 |
| Malv. | My prayers, minx! |
| Maria | No, I warrant you, he will not hear of godliness. |
| Malv. | Go, hang yourselves all! You are idle shallow things; I am not of your element; you shall know more hereafter. |

*Exit*

| Toby | Is it possible? |
| Fabian | If this were played upon a stage now, I could condemn it as an improbable fiction. |
| Toby | His very genius hath taken the infection of the device, man. 130 |
| Maria | Nay, pursue him now, lest the device take air and taint. |
| Fabian | Why, we shall make him mad indeed. |
| Maria | The house will be the quieter. |
| Toby | Come, we'll have him in a dark room and bound. My niece is already in the belief that he's mad. We may carry it thus for our pleasure and his penance, till our very pastime, tired out of breath, prompt us to have mercy on him; at which time we will bring the device to the bar and crown thee for 140 a finder of madmen. But see, but see! |

*Enter* Sir Andrew

| Fabian | More matter for a May morning! |
| Andrew | Here's the challenge; read it. I warrant there's vinegar and pepper in it. |
| Fabian | Is it so saucy? |
| Andrew | Ay, is it. I warrant him. Do but read. |

148    **scurvy:** *literally* 'full of scabs'—*hardly a valiant expression*

150    **admire:** wonder (*Sir Andrew repeats himself unknowingly.*)

152–153    **keeps . . . law:** 'makes sure that you will not be punished by the authorities' (*because there is no direct challenge*)

155    **liest in thy throat:** a more aggressive way of calling a person a liar (*After this, according to the rules, a fight was inevitable. What Cesario is supposed to have lied about, not even St Andrew knows.*)

         **in thy throat:** deeply

158–161    *While ensuring that Cesario sounds like the attacker, Sir Andrew innocently reveals how uncertain he is of his own fighting ability.*

162    **on the windy side:** on the right side (*just as a ship could sail to safety if its position was on the windward side*)

164–165    **my hope is better:** 'he will not need God's mercy if he is not killed'

165–166    **as thou usest him:** *a formal expression, like 'Yours sincerely' from an ordinary letter—oddly out of place in a challenge*

168    **his legs cannot:** 'then nothing can move him'

170    **fit occasion:** good chance (*One part of the plot fits neatly into another. Viola steps from one difficulty into another.*)

173    **scout me:** spy out the land (*Sir Toby is keen to get Sir Andrew out of the way so that he and Fabian can set up the mock-duel behind his back.*)

174    **bum-baily:** a sheriff's officer who would lie in wait to arrest debtors

175    **draw:** *his sword*

176–179    **for . . . earned him:** 'for it often happens that a hair-raising oath violently flung off in a boastful way works wonders by contrast with an actual brave deed, in making a man appear full of courage.'

| | |
|---|---|
| 'oby | Give me. '*Youth, whatsoever thou art, thou art but a scurvy fellow.*' |
| abian | Good, and valiant. |
| 'oby | '*Wonder not, nor admire not in thy mind why I do call* 150 *thee so, for I will show thee no reason for it.*' |
| abian | A good note, that keeps you from the blow of the law. |
| 'oby | '*Thou comest to the Lady Olivia, and in my sight she uses thee kindly; but thou liest in thy throat—that is not the matter I challenge thee for.*' |
| abian | Very brief, and to exceeding good sense—less. |
| Toby | '*I will waylay thee going home; where, if it be thy chance to kill me*'— |
| Fabian | Good.     160 |
| Toby | '*Thou killest me like a rogue and a villain.*' |
| Fabian | Still you keep on the windy side of the law; good. |
| Toby | '*Fare thee well, and God have mercy upon one of our souls. He may have mercy upon mine, but my hope is better, and so look to thyself. Thy friend as thou usest him, and thy sworn enemy,* |
| |                            *Andrew Aguecheek.*' If this letter move him not, his legs cannot. I'll give it him. |
| Maria | You may have very fit occasion for it; he is now in 170 some commerce with my lady, and will by and by depart. |
| Toby | Go, Sir Andrew; scout me for him at the corner of the orchard like a bum-baily. So soon as ever thou seest him, draw, and as thou drawest, swear horrible; for it comes to pass oft that a terrible oath, with a swaggering accent sharply twanged off, gives manhood more approbation, than ever |

| | |
|---|---|
| 180 | 'Just leave it to me; I'm an expert at swearing.' |
| 181–192 | 'You won't see me delivering his letter, for you can tell from the way Cesario behaves that he is intelligent and well brought up—just look at the way he is used as a messenger between Orsino and Olivia. Consequently, this letter, since it is so extraordinarily naïve, won't frighten Cesario one little bit: in fact, he will see it has been written by a blockhead. No, what I will do is to deliver the challenge in person, give Sir Andrew the reputation of being astonishingly brave, and so make Cesario—who in his inexperience will readily believe me—terrified at the thought of Sir Andrew's rage, skill and fierceness in fencing, and his eagerness to fight.' |
| 194 | **cockatrices:** mythical creatures—part snake, part cockerel—that could kill by a mere glance |
| 195 | **give them way:** keep out of their way |
| 196 | **presently:** straightaway (*The conspirators withdraw just out of earshot. Prose gives way to verse as Olivia reluctantly shows Cesario to the gate.*) |
| 199–203 | 'I have been too open in my appeals to your cold heart, and exposed my good name too rashly to it. A part of me keeps telling me I should be ashamed, but my feelings are so strong that it seems they laugh at my efforts to conquer them.' |
| 204–205 | 'My master is tormented (*by unrequited love*) in just the same way as you.' (*Viola is still trying to make Olivia love Orsino.*) |
| 204 | **bears:** produces |
| 206 | **jewel, picture:** a small portrait enclosed in a jewelled locket |

|            |                                                                                      |      |
|------------|--------------------------------------------------------------------------------------|------|
|            | proof itself would have earned him. Away.                                             |      |
| Andrew     | Nay, let me alone for swearing.                                                       | 180  |

*Exit*

| Toby   | Now will not I deliver his letter; for the behaviour of the young gentleman gives him out to be of good capacity and breeding; his employment between his lord and my niece confirms no less. Therefore, this letter, being so excellently ignor-ant, will breed no terror in the youth; he will find it comes from a clodpole. But, sir, I will deliver his challenge by word of mouth; set upon Aguecheek a notable report of valour, and drive the gentleman—as I know his youth will aptly 190 receive it—into a most hideous opinion of his rage, skill, fury and impetuosity. This will so fright them both that they will kill one another by the look, like cockatrices. |
|--------|--------------------------------------------------------------------------------------|

| Fabian | Here he comes with your niece; give them way till he take leave, and presently after him. |
|--------|-----------------------------------------------------------------------------------|

| Toby | I will meditate the while upon some horrid message for a challenge. |
|------|--------------------------------------------------------------------|

*Exeunt* Sir Toby, Fabian *and* Maria

*Enter* Olivia *and* Viola

| Olivia | I have said too much unto a heart of stone,<br>And laid mine honour too unchary on it.    200<br>There's something in me that reproves my fault;<br>But such a headstrong potent fault it is,<br>That it but mocks reproof. |
|--------|-----------------------------------------------------------------------------------------|

| Viola | With the same behaviour that your passion bears<br>Goes on my master's grief. |
|-------|----------------------------------------------------------------------|

| Olivia | Here, wear this jewel for me; 'tis my picture. |
|--------|-----------------------------------------------|

| | |
|---|---|
| 207 | **no tongue:** *It will not pester Cesario as Olivia does.* |
| 209–210 | 'I'll give you anything you care to ask for, provided m[ ] honour is not destroyed.' |
| 212 | **with mine honour:** honourably |
| 214 | **acquit:** release (*from her offered love*) |
| 216 | 'Even if you were a devil, I would go with you, even to hell[ ] |
| 217 | *Sir Toby plants himself in Cesario's way; he is now in complet[ ] control, Fabian an admiring assistant. He aims to catch Cesario o[ ] his guard by his vivid description of the 'ferocious' Sir Andrew. H[ ] avoids naming Cesario's opponent in case Cesario has heard of th[ ] cowardly Sir Andrew, and also to puzzle him by the vagueness of th[ ] quarrel.* |
| 219–224 | 'Get ready to defend yourself as best you can. I don't know what you have done to offend him, but the man lying i[ ] wait for you, brim full of defiance, and as eager for blood a[ ] a huntsman, is lurking at the end of the orchard. Draw you[ ] sword; get ready quickly for he fights with lightning speed and deadly accuracy.' |
| 226 | **to:** with |
| 226–227 | **my remembrance … man:** 'I cannot remember any occasion when I have given anyone offence.' (*Scared by Sir Toby's colloquial abruptness, Viola chooses her words carefully, to avoid offending him.*) |
| 230 | **opposite:** opponent |
| 233 | **what:** who (*Sir Toby avoids the direct answer.*) |
| 234–235 | **dubbed … consideration:** 'knighted, not on the field of battle, but at court on some peaceful occasion' (*Sir Toby is suggesting that Cesario will not have heard of his opponent's reputation in war, but he is, nevertheless, a dark horse.*) |

|  | Refuse it not; it hath no tongue to vex you. |
|  | And, I beseech you, come again tomorrow. |
|  | What shall you ask of me that I'll deny, |
|  | That honour, saved, may upon asking give? 210 |
| Viola | Nothing but this, your true love for my master. |
| Olivia | How, with mine honour, may I give him that, |
|  | Which I have given to you? |
| Viola | I will acquit you. |
| Olivia | Well, come again tomorrow. Fare thee well. |
|  | A fiend like thee might bear my soul to hell. |

*Exit*

*Enter* Sir Toby *and* Fabian

| Toby | Gentleman, God save thee. |
| Viola | And you, sir. |
| Toby | That defence thou hast, betake thee to it. Of what nature the wrongs are thou hast done him, 220 I know not; but thy interceptor, full of despite, bloody as the hunter, attends thee at the orchard end. Dismount thy tuck, be yare in thy preparation, for thy assailant is quick, skilful and deadly. |
| Viola | You mistake, sir, I am sure; no man hath any quarrel to me; my remembrance is very free and clear from any image of offence done to any man. |
| Toby | You'll find it otherwise, I assure you; therefore, if you hold your life at any price, betake you to your guard, for your opposite hath in him what 230 youth, strength, skill and wrath can furnish man withal. |
| Viola | I pray you, sir, what is he? |
| Toby | He is knight dubbed with unhatched rapier, and on carpet consideration, but he is a devil in private brawl. Souls and bodies hath he divorced |

237     **incensement:** rage

238–239     **that satisfaction . . . sepulchre:** *a melodramatic way of saying,* 'that he will be satisfied only when someone is dead and buried.'

239     **Hob, nob:** *an older, more vivid version of* 'give it or take it' —*i.e.,* 'come what may'

242     **conduct of:** escort provided by (*The comedy of this 'fight sequence' comes from the cowardice of the two opponents. Viola, being a girl, is naturally scared stiff. The audience can both laugh at her and, at the same time, sympathise with her.*)

242–245     **I have heard . . . quirk:** 'I have heard that there are some men who pick a quarrel with a person, just to test if he is brave; no doubt this man has that queer habit.'

246–252     'That's not the case with him: there must be a real insult to cause him to be angry. So you must go on and settle the matter in his way. I won't let you return to the house unless you first fight a duel with me—and that would be as dangerous as fighting him. So, on with you, or draw your sword against me; for you are going to have to fight in this affair, or, if you don't, you'll have to give up wearing a sword in shame.'

254–257     'I haven't the faintest idea why you are treating me so rudely. Please be so kind as to ask this gentleman how I have offended him; it must be something I have done by accident, and nothing intentional.' (*Viola is still trying desperately not to provoke Sir Toby.*)

258     *Fabian is left to make sure Cesario does not escape before Sir Toby fetches Sir Andrew.*

262     **mortal arbitrement:** fight to the death

265–266     **to read . . . form:** to judge by appearances (*Viola has already met Sir Andrew, and Fabian does not want her to lose her fear the moment Sir Toby brings in her combatant.*)

three, and his incensement at this moment is so
implacable that satisfaction can be none but by
pangs of death and sepulchre. Hob, nob, is his
word; give it or take it.                                    240

Viola        I will return again into the house, and desire some
conduct of the lady. I am no fighter. I have heard
of some kind of men that put quarrels purposely
on others, to taste their valour; belike, this is a
man of that quirk.

Toby        Sir, no. His indignation derives itself out of a very
competent injury; therefore get you on and give
him his desire. Back you shall not to the house,
unless you undertake that with me, which with
as much safety you might answer him. Therefore 250
on, or strip your sword stark naked; for meddle
you must, that's certain, or forswear to wear iron
about you.

Viola        This is as uncivil as strange. I beseech you, do me
this courteous office, as to know of the knight
what my offence to him is; it is something of my
negligence, nothing of my purpose.

Toby        I will do so. Signior Fabian, stay you by this
gentleman till my return.

*Exit*

Viola        Pray you, sir, do you know of this matter?        260

Fabian    I know the knight is incensed against you, even
to a mortal arbitrement, but nothing of the
circumstance more.

Viola        I beseech you, what manner of man is he?

Fabian    Nothing of that wonderful promise, to read him
by his form, as you are like to find him in the proof
of his valour. He is indeed, sir, the most skilful,

269–270    **Will you walk towards him?:** *Fabian does little more than echo Sir Toby, but his casualness is probably all the more frightening. Viola recoils from the idea of going to meet Sir Andrew and withdraws to discuss how Fabian can help her.*

272–273    **I am . . . knight:** 'I am all for peace' (*A clergyman's university degree allowed him to be called* 'Sir'.)

274    **of my mettle:** 'how brave I am' (*i.e., not brave at all*)

275–281    'I can tell you—he's a real devil; I've never seen such a furious creature ('firago' *is Sir Toby's version of* 'virago', *a fiery-tempered woman*). I took him on for a short bout with rapier etc. and he lunged through my defence with such deadly efficiency that there was no chance of stopping him. When you thrust at him in your turn he hits you back in a twinkling. I've heard he was the Shah of Persia's fencing instructor.' (*To Sir Andrew, anything is possible. Sir Toby demonstrates each stroke with his sword, to scare Sir Andrew out of his wits.*)

282    **Pox on it!:** A plague on it!

284    *They can just see across the stage that Fabian is holding on to Cesario, though not for this reason.*

286    **cunning in fence:** a skilled swordsman

287–288    **Let him . . . slip:** 'If he will overlook this affair'

290–292    'I'll put it to him. You stay here and cheer up. You'll see, it will all end without loss of life.'

293    **I ride you:** I make a fool of you (*Sir Toby sees the chance to trick Sir Andrew out of his horse.*)

294–295    *The plotters confer quickly while the combatants eye each other from a distance, then Sir Toby crosses to Cesario. Much of the comedy of this scene comes from the shuffling and circling of the four across the stage.*

|        | bloody and fatal opposite that you could possibly have found in any part of Illyria. Will you walk towards him? I will make your peace with him if 270 I can. |
|--------|---|
| Viola  | I shall be much bound to you for it. I am one that had rather go with sir priest than sir knight; I care not who knows so much of my mettle. |

*Exeunt*

*Enter* Sir Toby *and* Sir Andrew

| Toby | Why, man, he's a very devil! I have not seen such a firago. I had a pass with him, rapier, scabbard and all; and he gives me the stuck-in with such a mortal motion that it is inevitable; and, on the answer, he pays you as surely as your feet hit the ground they step on. They say he has been fencer 280 to the Sophy. |
|--------|---|
| Andrew | Pox on it! I'll not meddle with him. |
| Toby | Ay, but he will not now be pacified. Fabian can scarce hold him yonder. |
| Andrew | Plague on it! An I thought he had been valiant and so cunning in fence, I'd have seen him damned ere I'd have challenged him. Let him let the matter slip, and I'll give him my horse, grey Capilet. |
| Toby | I'll make the motion. Stand here, make a good 290 show of it; this shall end without the perdition of souls. (*aside*) Marry, I'll ride your horse as well as I ride you. |

*Enter* Fabian *and* Viola

(*to* Fabian) I have his horse to take up the quarrel. I have persuaded him the youth's a devil.

296     **conceited of:** terrified in his imagination about

298–303     'There's nothing we can do, Cesario; he's determined to fight so that he won't break his oath. Yet he has had second thoughts about the cause of the quarrel, and now realises there's nothing to it. All you have to do, then, is to flourish your sword a bit so that he can keep his oath. Don't worry— he's promised not to hurt you.' (*Sir Toby sees that both opponents are liable to surrender before the fight, so, to get them to draw their swords, he tells them both that the whole affair will only be light-hearted.*)

304     **A little thing:** It wouldn't take much to

309     **duello:** laws of duelling

313     *The audience is given a few comical manoeuvres with Fabian manipulating Cesario's sword and Sir Toby controlling Sir Andrew's, before Antonio rushes in to champion the presumed 'Sebastian' against Sir Andrew. Antonio, very naturally, mistakes Viola for her twin brother, Sebastian, as they are dressed identically.*

316     **for him:** on his behalf

320     **undertaker:** meddler (*undertaking Cesario's fight for him*)

320     **I am for you:** I'll fight you too

322     **anon:** presently (*Sir Toby is not very keen to clash with the officers of the law, and withdraws out of their way until they have finished their business. This gives Cesario and Sir Andrew a chance to make a pact.*)

| | |
|---|---|
| Fabian | He is as horribly conceited of him, and pants and looks pale, as if a bear were at his heels. |
| Toby | (*to* Viola) There's no remedy, sir; he will fight with you for his oath's sake. Marry, he hath better bethought him of his quarrel, and he finds that now scarce to be worth talking of. Therefore draw for the supportance of his vow; he protests he will not hurt you. |
| Viola | (*aside*) Pray God defend me! A little thing would make me tell them how much I lack of a man. |
| Fabian | Give ground if you see him furious. |
| Toby | Come, Sir Andrew, there's no remedy; the gentleman will for his honour's sake have one bout with you—he cannot by the duello avoid it; but he has promised me, as he is a gentleman and a soldier, he will not hurt you. Come on, to it. |
| Andrew | Pray God he keep his oath! |
| Viola | I do assure you 'tis against my will. |

*Viola and* Sir Andrew *draw their swords*

*Enter* Antonio

| | |
|---|---|
| Antonio | Put up your sword. If this young gentleman Have done offence, I take the fault on me; If you offend him, I for him defy you. |
| Toby | You, sir? Why, what are you? |
| Antonio | One, sir, that for his love dares yet do more Than you have heard him brag to you he will. |
| Toby | Nay, if you be an undertaker, I am for you. |

Sir Toby *and* Antonio *draw their swords*

| | |
|---|---|
| Fabian | O, good Sir Toby, hold; here come the officers. |
| Toby | I'll be with you anon. |

325    **He:** Sir Andrew's horse (*Viola, of course, has no idea what he is talking about.*)

326    **reins well:** is easy to ride

327    **do thy office:** do what you're paid to do

328    **at the suit:** in the name

330    **no jot:** not at all

       **favour:** face

332    *The Officer has recognised Antonio from the previous sea-fight.*

335    **answer:** face up to the penalty

336–337    **my necessity . . . purse:** 'because I shall need it, I shall have to ask you for my purse' (*Even in his misfortune, Antonio thinks more of how his friend will be affected.*)

342    *Antonio has to repeat his request. 'Sebastian' is apparently too stunned to understand.*

343–350    'What are you talking about? Out of gratitude for your kindness to me just now, and out of pity for your present misfortune, I'll lend you some of the little money I have. I have very little indeed, but I'll give you half of what I've got on me. There you are—half my wealth.'

352–353    'Haven't I done enough for you?'

| | |
|---|---|
| Viola | Pray, sir, put your sword up if you please. |
| Andrew | Marry will I, sir; and for that I promised you, I'll be as good as my word. He will bear you easily and reins well. |

*Enter two* Officers

| | | |
|---|---|---|
| 1 Off. | This is the man; do thy office. | |
| 2 Off. | Antonio, I arrest thee at the suit of Count Orsino. | |
| Antonio | You do mistake me, sir. | |
| 1 Off. | No, sir, no jot; I know your favour well, | 330 |
| | Though now you have no sea-cap on your head. | |
| | Take him away; he knows I know him well. | |
| Antonio | I must obey. | |
| | (*to* Viola) This comes with seeking you. | |
| | But there's no remedy; I shall answer it. | |
| | What will you do, now my necessity | |
| | Makes me to ask you for my purse? It grieves me | |
| | Much more for what I cannot do for you | |
| | Than what befalls myself. You stand amazed, | |
| | But be of comfort. | 340 |
| 2 Off. | Come, sir, away. | |
| Antonio | I must entreat of you some of that money. | |
| Viola | What money, sir? | |
| | For the fair kindness you have showed me here, | |
| | And part being prompted by your present trouble, | |
| | Out of my lean and low ability | |
| | I'll lend you something. My having is not much; | |
| | I'll make division of my present with you. | |
| | Hold, there's half my coffer. | 350 |
| Antonio | Will you deny me now? | |
| | Is it possible that my deserts to you | |
| | Can lack persuasion? Do not tempt my misery, | |

354     **unsound:** desperate

355     **upbraid:** reproach (*by reminding 'Sebastian' about them*)

361–362     'Or any of the forms evil takes to enter our weak bodies' (*Antonio cries out against what seems horrible hypocrisy. His bitter words are one more trial for Viola. Again she is ignorant what it is all about, but, this time, there is a ray of hope for her.*)

367–370     'I saved him when he was half-drowned and comforted him with the purest form of love. I devoted myself to him because he seemed to be a man who deserved such respect ('venerable worth').' (*Antonio's language suggests worship—'sanctity', 'image', 'venerable', 'devotion'; Sebastian was his idol, but now Antonio has found his idol has feet of clay.*)

373–377     'Sebastian, you have disgraced your good looks. A person's cruel mind, not his deformed ugly body, is the one thing which ruins his nature. Virtue is the true form that beauty takes, but beauty is not always a sign of virtue; an attractive person who is also evil is like an empty treasure-chest which the devil has carved on the outside with cunning decorations.' (*This is serious moralising coming unexpectedly at the end of a scene of farcical comedy. It is as much for the audience's benefit as for a warning to Antonio. Both are being reminded of what Viola had said at the beginning of the play: that appearances are deceptive, and that a person's character is to be judged by his actions.*)

381–384     'I think he is so worked up that he really believes what he says. It's the same with me, isn't it? (Am I just willing myself to believe Antonio has mistaken me for Sebastian?) I pray that I am not dreaming and that I have been mistaken, Sebastian, for you.'

|         | Lest that it make me so unsound a man |      |
|---------|----------------------------------------|------|
|         | As to upbraid you with those kindnesses |      |
|         | That I have done for you.               |      |
| Viola   | I know of none;                         |      |
|         | Nor know I you by voice or any feature. |      |
|         | I hate ingratitude more in a man        |      |
|         | Than lying, vainness, babbling drunkenness, | 360 |
|         | Or any taint of vice whose strong corruption |  |
|         | Inhabits our frail blood.               |      |
| Antonio | O heavens themselves!                   |      |
| 2 Off.  | Come, sir, I pray you go.               |      |
| Antonio | Let me speak a little.                  |      |
|         | This youth that you see here            |      |
|         | I snatched one half out of the jaws of death, |  |
|         | Relieved him with such sanctity of love, |     |
|         | And to his image, which methought did promise |  |
|         | Most venerable worth, did I devotion.   | 370  |
| 1 Off.  | What's that to us? The time goes by; away. |  |
| Antonio | But O, how vile an idol proves this god! |    |
|         | Thou hast, Sebastian, done good feature shame. |  |
|         | In nature there's no blemish but the mind; |   |
|         | None can be called deformed but the unkind. |  |
|         | Virtue is beauty, but the beauteous-evil |    |
|         | Are empty trunks o'erflourished by the devil. |  |
| 1 Off.  | The man grows mad; away with him! Come, come, sir. |  |
| Antonio | Lead me on.                             | 380  |

*Exit with* Officers

| Viola | Methinks his words do from such passion fly |
|-------|---------------------------------------------|
|       | That he believes himself—so do not I?       |
|       | Prove true, imagination, O prove true,      |

386      **couplet:** *Sir Toby has not heard Viola's last words but is joking about the couplets delivered by Antonio as he was dragged off. To Sir Toby they were pompous old proverbs, 'sage saws'.*

387–391      **I my . . . imitate:** 'In a sense, I keep my brother alive: I look in the mirror and see him. He was just like this in appearance and he always used to dress in this style and colour with decoration like this on his clothes. It's from him that I got the idea for my costume.' (*In case the audience should wonder why the twins are dressed identically, here is the explanation.*)

391      **if it prove:** if it is true (*that Sebastian has survived*)

392      *Viola has had no chance to question Antonio; the comedy and suffering caused by the confusion between the twins is not yet over; but she goes out this time full of hope, quite forgetting the other characters.*

393      **more a coward:** a bigger coward

397      'An utter coward dedicated to being a coward.'

398      **'Slid:** a common oath; a corruption of 'by God's eyelid' (*Sir Andrew would keep inside the law if he just struck Cesario with his fist.*)

402      'I bet you anything it will all come to nothing.' (*Sir Toby is afraid this joke has fizzled out, but he is prepared to make a last effort to keep it alive. When Sebastian immediately enters, the audience anticipates with some satisfaction the arrival of Sir Andrew with his newly discovered 'bravery'.*)

|        | That I, dear brother, be now taken for you! |
|--------|---------------------------------------------|
| Toby   | Come hither, knight; come hither, Fabian. We'll whisper o'er a couplet or two of most sage saws. |
| Viola  | He named Sebastian. I my brother know |

Viola    Yet living in my glass; even such and so
In favour was my brother, and he went
Still in this fashion, colour, ornament;      390
For him I imitate. O, if it prove,
Tempests are kind and salt waves fresh in love!

*Exit*

| Toby   | A very dishonest paltry boy, and more a coward than a hare. His dishonesty appears in leaving his friend here in necessity and denying him; and, for his cowardship, ask Fabian. |
| Fabian | A coward, a most devout coward, religious in it. |
| Andrew | 'Slid, I'll after him again and beat him. |
| Toby   | Do; cuff him soundly, but never draw thy sword. |
| Andrew | An I do not—                      400 |

*Exit*

| Fabian | Come, let's see the event. |
| Toby   | I dare lay any money 'twill be nothing yet. |

*Exeunt*

Sebastian and Feste enter arguing. Feste is scornful, thinking he is talking to the polite gentle Cesario. Sebastian's forceful impatience with the Clown is a strong contrast to his sister's behaviour in Act 3, Scene 1. This conversation at cross-purposes puts him in the right mood to turn on Sir Andrew and Sir Toby when they provoke him.

3    **Go to:** Clear off

5    **held out:** kept up (*the supposed pretence of not knowing Feste and why he has been sent after 'Cesario'. Feste's series of negatives are heavy with sarcasm.*)

9    'Nothing is really what it is.'

10    **vent thy folly:** go and play the fool (*It is Feste's trade to pick at words. He seizes upon the unusual word 'vent' meaning 'utter'.*)

12    **of:** spoken by

14–15    **this great . . . cockney:** 'everybody nowadays is going in for affected speech'
       **lubber:** any clumsy fellow
       **cockney:** effeminate dandy with an affected way of speaking

15–16    **ungird thy strangeness:** 'stop pretending that you don't know me' (*Feste replies with a similarly affected expression.*)

18    **Greek:** a clown who talks gibberish

20    **worse payment:** *by striking him*

21–23    'You are generous—I'll say that for you. Just consider how intelligent men give their money away to fools to buy themselves a high reputation (*among fools*), but what an exorbitant price they pay (14 years' rent to buy a piece of land)!' (*This is not the first money the supposed 'Cesario' has given Feste, and he is surprised how little he has had to do for it.*)

24    *Without ceremony, Sir Andrew rushes to the attack, now that he thinks he is dealing with a bigger coward than himself.*

# ACT 4

SCENE 1   Outside Olivia's house
*Enter* Sebastian *and* Feste.

Feste     Will you make me believe that I am not sent for
          you?

Sebas.    Go to, go to; thou art a foolish fellow. Let me be
          clear of thee.

Feste     Well held out, in faith! No, I do not know you,
          nor I am not sent to you by my lady, to bid you
          come speak with her; nor your name is not
          Master Cesario, nor this is not my nose neither.
          Nothing that is so is so.

Sebas.    I prithee, vent thy folly somewhere else; thou      10
          knowest not me.

Feste     Vent my folly! He has heard that word of some
          great man, and now applies it to a fool. Vent my
          folly! I am afraid this great lubber, the world,
          will prove a cockney. I prithee now, ungird thy
          strangeness and tell me what I shall vent to my
          lady. Shall I vent to her that thou art coming?

Sebas.    I prithee, foolish Greek, depart from me. There's
          money for thee; if you tarry longer, I shall give
          worse payment.                                      20

Feste     By my troth, thou hast an open hand. These wise
          men that give fools money get themselves a good
          report—after fourteen years' purchase.

          *Enter* Sir Andrew

Andrew    Now, sir, have I met you again? There's for you.
          (*striking* Sebastian)

27    *Sebastian has knocked Sir Andrew down with the flat side of his dagger. Sir Toby grabs hold of him and pulls him away from Sir Andrew.*

28    **straight:** at once (*Feste presumably knows of Olivia's concern for Cesario and knows how cross she will be when she hears that he has been attacked. He cannot risk her thinking he is an accomplice of Sir Toby's.*)

30    **hold:** stop struggling

31    **work:** deal

32–33 **I'll have . . . against him:** 'I'll bring a case of assault against him' (*Sir Andrew doesn't realise that he would have no case, because as he admits, he was the aggressor—he is quite determined that he has had enough of fighting.*)

37    **put . . . fleshed:** 'sheathe your sword; you have tasted enough blood'

42    **malapert:** cheeky

45    **Ungracious wretch:** *Olivia is furious with Sir Toby—so her attack on him as some species of primitive man is out of all proportion to what he has done. He depends on her for his board and lodging, so he cannot argue but only slink off.*

50    **Rudesby:** ruffian (*flung at the retreating Sir Toby*)

| Sebas. | Why, there's for thee, and there, and there! Are all the people mad? (*beating* Sir Andrew) |
|---|---|

*Enter* Sir Toby *and* Fabian

| Toby | Hold sir, or I'll throw your dagger o'er the house. |
|---|---|
| Feste | This will I tell my lady straight, I would not be in some of your coats for twopence. |

*Exit*

| Toby | Come on, sir, hold. | 30 |
|---|---|---|
| Andrew | Nay, let him alone. I'll go another way to work with him; I'll have an action of battery against him, if there be any law in Illyria. Though I struck him first, yet it's no matter for that. |
| Sebas. | Let go thy hand. |
| Toby | Come, sir, I will not let you go. Come, my young soldier, put up your iron; you are well fleshed. Come on. |
| Sebas. | I will be free from thee. What wouldst thou now? If thou darest tempt me further, draw thy sword. | 40 |
| Toby | What, what! Nay then, I must have an ounce or two of this malapert blood from you. |

*Enter* Olivia

| Olivia | Hold, Toby! On thy life, I charge thee, hold! |
|---|---|
| Toby | Madam! |
| Olivia | Will it be ever thus? Ungracious wretch. Fit for the mountains and the barbarous caves, Where manners ne'er were preached! Out of my sight! Be not offended, dear Cesario. Rudesby, be gone. | 50 |

*Exeunt* Sir Toby, Sir Andrew *and* Fabian

52–60  'Don't be angry, but try to think calmly and sensibly about this crude unprovoked attack on your life. Come into the house with me and there I'll tell you about all the stupid practical jokes this ruffian keeps getting up. Then you'll be able to see how comical it all is. I won't take no for an answer: so don't say anything. Confound the man! He startled my heart, which I had given to you, when he struck at your heart.'

61–64  'What is it all about? How is it going to end? Either I am mad or I must be dreaming. May love drown for ever my powers of reasoning. If dreams are all like this, then may I always remain asleep.' (*Sebastian turns away from Olivia bewildered, then decides to chance his luck and go with her.*)

63  **Lethe:** the river in the underworld whose water made you forget your memories of mortal life (*A minute ago, Sebastian thought everyone else must be mad. Now he is less sure, because he hopes Olivia is sane.*)

65  **would thou'dst:** I wish you would

## Scene 2

Time is rapidly running short. With Sebastian's arrival, it cannot be long before the confusion over Viola's identity is brought to a head. Even the conspiracy against Malvolio has to be ended quickly, for Sir Toby feels he has gone too far this time and is in danger of being thrown out of the house. This scene, then, is Feste's chance to be revenged on Malvolio for trying to set Olivia against him in Act 1, Scene 5. All attention is centred on him as he gaily dances to and fro in front of the dark room enclosing Malvolio.

1  *Once more it is Maria who organises the mischief. The disguise is unnecessary, since Malvolio cannot see Feste, but it helps to remind the audience of the impersonation.*

2  **Topas:** *probably chosen as the priest's name because the topaz stone was believed to cure madness*

3  **the whilst:** meanwhile

4–10  'Very well, I'll put it on and disguise myself. It would be

I prithee, gentle friend,
Let thy fair wisdom not thy passion, sway
In this uncivil and unjust extent
Against thy peace. Go with me to my house,
And hear thou there how many fruitless pranks
This ruffian hath botched up, that thou thereby
May'st smile at this.
Thou shalt not choose but go.
Do not deny. Beshrew his soul for me!
He started one poor heart of mine in thee.     60

Sebas.   What relish is in this? How runs the stream?
Or I am mad, or else this is a dream.
Let fancy still my sense in Lethe steep;
If it be thus to dream, still let me sleep!

Olivia   Nay, come, I prithee; would thou'dst be ruled
by me!

Sebas.   Madam, I will.

Olivia   O say so, and so be!

*Exeunt*


SCENE 2   Outside a room in Olivia's house
*Enter* Maria *and* Feste.


Maria   Nay, I prithee, put on this gown and this beard;
make him believe thou art Sir Topas, the curate;
do it quickly. I'll call Sir Toby the whilst.

*Exit*

Feste   Well, I'll put it on, and I will dissemble myself
in it, and I would I were the first that ever dis-
sembled in such a gown. I am not tall enough to

nice to think that I was the first man ever to pretend to be holy. I am not tall enough to look dignified like a priest, and I am not thin enough to look like a scholar (*scholars were always thought to be poor and underfed*)—but if people know that you are honest and that you always welcome them into your house, that's just as good as being close with your money and very learned.' (*He is criticising certain clergy for their hypocrisy in saying that they cannot afford to be generous.*)

11   'Here they come—the other members in the plot.'

13   **Bonos dies:** Feste's version of the Latin for 'Good-day' *This mock-learning is more of Feste's nonsense. The identity of the hermit and the king's niece is of no importance. In its simplest form all that Feste says is: 'I am what I seem to be—a parson.' In fact, it is one more example of things not being what they appear to be.*

19   *Feste puts on a parsonical voice.*

     **Peace in this prison:** *He prays for the house as though it were smitten with the plague.*

26   **Out, hyperbolical fiend:** *He tries to drive out the devil in Malvolio, as a priest might.*

     **hyperbolical:** given to exaggerated language (*more of Feste's nonsensical 'learning'*)

32   **dishonest:** lying

33   **modest:** mild

35   *Feste tries to make Malvolio doubt the evidence of his own senses; so far in the play he has always been convinced that he was right. From where Malvolio is, everything is black, but Feste pretends that he has said that the whole house is in darkness. He starts to refute this, but his reasoning is deliberate nonsense to confuse the already bewildered Malvolio.*

become the function well, nor lean enough to be thought a good student; but to be said an honest man and a good housekeeper goes as fairly as to say, a careful man and a great scholar. 10

The competitors enter.

*Enter* Sir Toby *and* Maria

| | |
|---|---|
| Toby | Jove bless thee, Master Parson. |
| Feste | *Bonos dies*, Sir Toby; for, as the old hermit of Prague, that never saw pen and ink, very wittily said to a niece of King Gorboduc, 'That that is, is'; so I, being Master Parson, am Master Parson; for what is 'that' but 'that', and 'is' but 'is'? |
| Toby | To him, Sir Topas. |
| Feste | What ho, I say! Peace in this prison! |
| Toby | The knave counterfeits well; a good knave. 20 |
| Malv. | (*within*) Who calls there? |
| Feste | Sir Topas, the curate, who comes to visit Malvolio, the lunatic. |
| Malv. | Sir Topas, Sir Topas, good Sir Topas, go to my lady. |
| Feste | Out, hyperbolical fiend! How vexest thou this man! Talkest thou nothing but of ladies? |
| Toby | Well said, Master Parson. |
| Malv. | Sir Topas, never was man thus wronged. Good Sir Topas, do not think I am mad; they have laid 30 me here in hideous darkness. |
| Feste | Fie, thou dishonest Satan! I call thee by the most modest terms, for I am one of those gentle ones that will use the devil himself with courtesy. Sayest thou that house is dark? |
| Malv. | As hell, Sir Topas. |

37–40    'Why, the house's bay windows let through as much light as a barricade (*i.e., none*), and the upper windows at the south-north end (*wherever that is!*) are as bright as black wood. Despite this, do you still say that something is blocking the light?'

43    *This is the first time Feste has spoken to Malvolio as distinct from the supposed devil inside Malvolio. His words still are in character with a priest.*

45    **fog:** the darkness that covered Egypt, as Moses' 9th plague

48    **thus abused:** so badly treated

49–50    **in any constant question:** 'by testing me on some serious philosophical matter'

51    *Feste sees the chance to insult Malvolio if he asks him to discuss the Greek Pythagoras' philosophy that the human soul passes at a man's death into the body of some animal or bird, 'wild fowl'.*

53–54    'That one's grandmother's soul might perhaps have been transferred to a bird.'

56    **no way approve:** do not in the least believe in (*Malvolio's reply is that of any normal, sane Christian.*)

60    **allow of thy wits:** pass you as sane

      **woodcock:** the bird noted for its silliness (*so Feste is indirectly insulting Malvolio's grandmother*)

61    **dispossess:** turn it out of its place of rest

63    *Malvolio calls desperately after Feste as he slips away to his admiring audience.*

65    **I am for all waters:** I can turn my hand to anything

| | |
|---|---|
| Feste | Why, it hath bay windows transparent as barricadoes, and the clerestories toward the south-north are as lustrous as ebony; and yet complainest thou of obstruction? 40 |
| Malv. | I am not mad, Sir Topas; I say to you this house is dark. |
| Feste | Madman, thou errest. I say there is no darkness but ignorance, in which thou art more puzzled than the Egyptians in their fog. |
| Malv. | I say this house is as dark as ignorance, though ignorance were as dark as hell: and I say there was never man thus abused. I am no more mad than you are. Make the trial of it in any constant question. 50 |
| Feste | What is the opinion of Pythagoras concerning wild fowl? |
| Malv. | That the soul of our grandam might haply inhabit a bird. |
| Feste | What thinkest thou of his opinion? |
| Malv. | I think nobly of the soul, and no way approve his opinion. |
| Feste | Fare thee well. Remain thou still in darkness. Thou shalt hold the opinion of Pythagoras ere I will allow of thy wits, and fear to kill a woodcock, 60 lest thou dispossess the soul of thy grandam. Fare thee well. |
| Malv. | Sir Topas, Sir Topas! |
| Toby | My most exquisite Sir Topas! |
| Feste | Nay, I am for all waters. |
| Maria | Thou mightst have done this without thy beard and gown; he sees thee not. |

68     **bring me word:** *Sir Toby is keen to be off, in case Olivia comes upon him in her present mood.*

69–74     'I wish we had got this roguery of ours out of the way. If we can find a convenient way of releasing him, we had better take it. The trouble is that I'm now so deeply in disgrace with Olivia that I daren't play this joke out to the full. Come as soon as you can to my room.'

75     *The easiest way for Malvolio to recognise Feste is by part of his clown's routine, so Feste pretends to be rehearsing one of his songs. The song is not as irrelevant as it may appear, for Malvolio too has lost his lady to another lover.*

78     **perdy:** truly

84     **Good fool:** *The wheel has come full circle, for Malvolio to have to flatter Feste.*

84–85     **as ever . . . hand:** 'if you want to be my friend for life'

88     *Feste pretends to be surprised that Malvolio is locked up in the house.*

90     'Is it really you, sir? How did you become mad?'

91     **notoriously:** shamefully

95     **propertied me:** 'stored me away, like an unwanted piece of stage property'

97     **face:** impudently drive

| Toby | To him in thine own voice, and bring me word how thou findest him. I would we were well rid of this knavery. If he may be conveniently delivered, 70 I would he were, for I am so far in offence with my niece that I cannot pursue with any safety this sport to the upshot. Come by and by to my chamber. |
|---|---|

*Exeunt* Sir Toby *and* Maria

| Feste | (*sings*) Hey, Robin, jolly Robin. |
|---|---|
| |     Tell me how thy lady does. |
| Malv. | Fool! |
| Feste |     My lady is unkind, perdy. |
| Malv. | Fool! |
| Feste |     Alas, why is she so? 80 |
| Malv. | Fool, I say! |
| Feste |     She loves another. |
| |     Who calls, ha? |
| Malv. | Good fool, as ever thou wilt deserve well at my hand, help me to a candle, and pen, ink and paper. As I am a gentleman, I will live to be thankful to thee for it. |
| Feste | Master Malvolio! |
| Malv. | Ay, good fool. |
| Feste | Alas, sir, how fell you besides your five wits! 90 |
| Malv. | Fool, there was never man so notoriously abused. I am as well in my wits, fool, as thou art. |
| Feste | But as well? Then you are mad indeed, if you be no better in your wits than a fool. |
| Malv. | They have here propertied me, keep me in darkness, send ministers to me—asses—and do all they can to face me out of my wits. |

| | |
|---|---|
| 98 | **Advise you:** Be careful (*To prove how versatile he is, Feste flits from one side of Malvolio's window to the other, changing his voice each time to keep up the imaginary conversation.*) |
| 101 | **endeavour thyself:** do your best |
| 102 | **vain bibble-babble:** idle babbling |
| 104 | **Maintain no words:** Do not talk |
| 112 | *Feste calls out politely after the 'departing' Sir Topas, then returns to Malvolio who is desperate lest he lose his one apparent friend.* |
| 113 | **shent:** told off |
| 117 | 'Alas, I only wish you were.' |
| 118 | **By this hand:** *all that Feste can see of Malvolio, who is clinging to the window bars* |
| 120–121 | **It shall . . . did:** 'You will be far better rewarded for this than for any other letter you may have carried in the past.' |
| 123 | **counterfeit:** pretend to be mad (*a neat way of insulting Malvolio, by saying that he gives the appearance of being mad*) |
| 127 | **requite . . . degree:** 'reward you in the most generous way I can' |

| | |
|---|---|
| Feste | (*in his own voice*) Advise you what you say; the minister is here. |
| | (*as* Sir Topas) Malvolio, Malvolio, thy wits the 100 heavens restore; endeavour thyself to sleep, and leave thy vain bibble-babble. |
| Malv. | Sir Topas! |
| Feste | (*as* Sir Topas) Maintain no words with him, good fellow. |
| | (*in his own voice*) Who? I, sir? Not I, sir. God be with you, good Sir Topas. |
| | (*as* Sir Topas) Marry, amen. |
| | (*in his own voice*) I will, sir, I will. |
| Malv. | Fool, fool, fool, I say! 110 |
| Feste | (*to* Malvolio) Alas, sir, be patient! |
| | (*to* Sir Topas) What say you, sir? |
| | (*to* Malvolio) I am shent for speaking to you. |
| Malv. | Good fool, help me to some light and some paper; I tell thee, I am as well in my wits as any man in Illyria. |
| Feste | Well-a-day, that you were, sir! |
| Malv. | By this hand, I am. Good fool, some ink, paper and light; and convey what I will set down to my lady. It shall advantage thee more than ever the 120 bearing of letter did. |
| Feste | I will help you to it. But tell me true, are you not mad indeed, or do you but counterfeit? |
| Malv. | Believe me, I am not, I tell thee true. |
| Feste | Nay, I'll ne'er believe a madman till I see his brains. I will fetch you light and paper and ink. |
| Malv. | Fool, I'll requite it in the highest degree. I prithee, be gone. |

129 *Feste alters a traditional song to make it refer insultingly to Malvolio. In the old Morality plays the popular impish figure, called the 'Vice', made fun of the devil, sometimes by cutting the devil's talons*—'paring his nails'—*with his thin wooden dagger*—'dagger of lath'. *So Feste has tricked his particular version of the devil and cut him down to size.*

133 **old:** old-fashioned

134 **your need to sustain:** to carry out your business

140 **goodman:** fellow (*a scornful word for Malvolio*)


## Scene 3

The audience has this last chance to give its approval to the man Olivia is to marry. It must not seem that she is being given a mere consolation prize because she cannot have Cesario. She rushes Sebastian into a binding engagement, which is both in keeping with her character—she cannot afford to let him have second thoughts—and, also, is an action which needs to be over before the closing scene. This marriage is the final straw which looks like forcing Viola to reveal her secret.

1 *Sebastian is still bewildered and is wondering whether his other senses are working properly.*

2 **This pearl:** *Sebastian is holding in his hand Olivia's gift. His ready acceptance of it contrasts with Viola's refusal of Olivia's other love-tokens.*

3 'though I am filled with amazement'

7 **was:** had been

  **credit:** general belief

9 **do me golden service:** would be most valuable to me (*Sebastian's first surprise has been Antonio's failure to be at their meeting-place.*)

10–24 'Commonsense ('my soul') tells me—although I long to be proved wrong—that there must be some mistake here, and that it is not true that Olivia is mad. Yet what has just happened to me ('this accident') and this overwhelming good fortune are so much beyond anything that has ever happened

Feste    (*sings*) I am gone, sir,

                And anon, sir,                             130

                I'll be with you again;

                    In a trice.

                    Like to the old vice,

                Your need to sustain;

                Who with dagger of lath,

                In his rage and his wrath,

                    Cries 'Ah ha!' to the devil

                Like a mad lad.

                Pare thy nails, dad;

                    Adieu, goodman devil.             140

                                        *Exit*

SCENE 3   Olivia's garden

*Enter* Sebastian.

Sebas.       This is the air; that is the glorious sun;

          This pearl she gave me, I do feel it and see it;

          And though 'tis wonder that enwraps me thus,

          Yet 'tis not madness.

              Where's Antonio then?

          I could not find him at the Elephant,

          Yet there he was, and there I found this credit,

          That he did range the town to seek me out.

          His counsel now might do me golden service.

              For though my soul disputes well with my     10

          sense

          That this may be some error but no madness,

          Yet doth this accident and flood of fortune

          So far exceed all instance, all discourse,

          That I am ready to distrust mine eyes

          And wrangle with my reason, that persuades me

before ('all instance') or that could reasonably happen to anyone ('all discourse',) that I am prepared to ignore the evidence of my eyes, and contradict my commonsense that tries to convince me of anything other than that either I am mad or Olivia is. On the other hand, if Olivia really were mad she wouldn't be able to control her household and order her servants about, attend to business matters and see that they are carried out—and all this in such a dignified way without the least fuss—as I can see she does. There must be something here that I've overlooked.' (*Sebastian does not want to believe Olivia is mad, but it seems the only explanation; yet he feels rightly that he has not fully understood the situation.*)

28    **chantry by:** chapel near by

30    *This is a formal engagement ceremony, prior to marriage, but one which was almost as binding as the marriage itself. Olivia can consider Sebastian her 'husband' after this occasion.*

31–35    'To settle my mind which is full of doubts and suspicions (*that she will lose him before they are united in marriage*). The priest will keep it a secret until you want it to be announced publicly, and then we shall celebrate it in a manner suited to my rank.' (*Olivia thinks 'Cesario' is frightened of Orsino's inevitable anger; she understands his caution and is prepared to wait.*)

40    **fairly note:** look kindly upon (*Olivia perhaps feels the need to ask for heaven's blessing when she is so blatantly rejecting her vow of 7 years' seclusion. Sebastian agrees with her wishes as though he were still in a dream world.*)

To any other trust but that I am mad,
Or else the lady's mad; yet, if 'twere so,
She could not sway her house, command her
followers,                                                    20
Take and give back affairs and their dispatch
With such a smooth, discreet and stable bearing
As I perceive she does. There's something in it
That is deceivable.
    But here the lady comes.

*Enter* Olivia *and* Priest

Olivia    Blame not this haste of mine. If you mean well,
Now go with me and with this holy man
Into the chantry by. There, before him,
And underneath that consecrated roof,
Plight me the full assurance of your faith,                    30
That my most jealous and too doubtful soul
May live at peace. He shall conceal it
Whiles you are willing it shall come to note,
What time we will our celebration keep
According to my birth. What do you say?

Sebas.    I'll follow this good man and go with you,
And, having sworn truth, ever will be true.

Olivia    Then lead the way, good father; and heavens so
shine
That they may fairly note this act of mine!                    40

                                                *Exeunt*

The audience has had a long wait for the meeting of Oliv
and Orsino. Olivia has suffered for her original haughtines
It is about time Orsino was jolted out of his dream an
made to face reality. Yet, just to reassure the audience tha
the world of Illyria need not be taken too seriously, Fes
acts as a kind of master of ceremonies, beginning and closir
the final scene.

1    *Malvolio's letter has been written and is going to be delivered*
     *Feste's convenience. For the time being, the audience can forget t*
     *subplot.*

2    **another:** in return

5–6  *A reference to a popular anecdote about Queen Elizabeth, who begge*
     *a favourite dog from a Dr. Bullein. In return he was granted a*
     *request; so he asked for the return of his dog.*

8    *Feste is mockingly humble.*

9    *Orsino is in the best of moods, having come to deliver in person h*
     *message of love to Olivia. He is, therefore, prepared to spend an id*
     *minute listening to the banter of Feste who has already entertaine*
     *him at his house.*

13   **Just the contrary:** 'Surely you mean the other way roun*

16–22 *Feste delights in a paradox. His point is that it is better to be awa*
     *of your faults (which enemies will tell you of) and so be able to corre*
     *them, than to be deceived into thinking you have no faults, by you*
     *friends' flattery.*

16   **make an ass of me:** *by, in fact, deceiving him about himself*

19   **abused:** deceived

20   **conclusions . . . kisses:** 'if points in an argument can b*
     treated like kissing' (*when, if a girl says 'no' four times, th*
     *negatives cancel each other out, and she means 'yes—yes'*)

20–21 *His reasoning contains four apparent denials of sense, which h*
     *playfully suggests add up to two good reasons.*

23   *Orsino admires Feste's skill with words, if not the truth of what h*
     *says.*

# ACT 5

SCENE 1   Outside Olivia's house
*Enter* Feste *and* Fabian.

Fabian   Now as thou lovest me, let me see his letter.

Feste   Good Master Fabian, grant me another request.

Fabian   Anything.

Feste   Do not desire to see this letter.

Fabian   This is to give a dog and, in recompense, desire
my dog again.

*Enter* Duke, Viola, Curio *and lords*

Duke   Belong you to the Lady Olivia, friends?

Feste   Ay, sir, we are some of her trappings.

Duke   I know thee well; how doest thou, my good
fellow?                                                                10

Feste   Truly, sir, the better for my foes and the worse
for my friends.

Duke   Just the contrary; the better for thy friends.

Feste   No, sir, the worse.

Duke   How can that be?

Feste   Marry, sir, they praise me and make an ass of me;
now my foes tell me plainly I am an ass; so that
by my foes, sir, I profit in the knowledge of
myself, and by my friends I am abused; so that,
conclusions to be as kisses, if your four negatives        20
make your two affirmatives, why then, the worse
for my friends and the better for my foes.

Duke   Why, this is excellent.

Feste   By my troth, sir, no; though it please you to be

| | |
|---|---|
| 25 | **one of my friends**: *by praising him, and so deceiving him* |
| 27 | **double-dealing**: *a pun on* doubling the amount of money given to Feste *and* cheating |
| 30-31 | 'Be generous and for once do what you feel like doing (and give me more money).' (*Feste puns on the three meanings of* 'your grace': '*your lordship*', '*generosity*', '*virtue*'. *Orsino good-naturedly allows the pun to win Feste more money, and so Feste tries again to see if his luck still holds.*) |
| 32 | **to be**: *as to be* |
| 34-38 | *By reeling off a jumble of things that are composed of threes, Feste hopes to add a third coin to his collection.* |
| 34 | **Primo . . . tertio**: *Latin for* 1st, 2nd, 3rd |
| 35 | **the third pays for all**: *a proverb meaning much the same as* third time lucky |
| | **triplex**: *a musical term*—a rhythm of three beats in a bar |
| 36 | **a good tripping measure**: a good rhythm to dance to |
| 36-37 | **Saint Bennet**: the church of St. Bennet Hithe was opposite the Globe Theatre |
| 40 | **throw**: occasion (*throw of the dice; Feste has been lucky twice*) |
| 42 | **awake my bounty**: make me feel generous again |
| 43-44 | **lullaby . . . again**: 'let your generosity go to sleep until I get back' (*so that no one else will be given the money Feste feels is almost his. He seizes on the metaphor of sleep from Orsino's using the word* 'awake'.) |
| 45 | **my desire of having**: my eagerness for money |
| 47 | **anon**: soon |
| 48 | *Antonio's arrival is not accidental. The officers who arrested him have sought out Orsino, who is both the ruler of Illyria, and a man with a personal grievance against the man. His punishment would depend on Orsino. It is a brief reminder that Orsino has interests and responsibilities outside the narrow circle which he has drawn for himself round Olivia.* |
| 51 | **Vulcan**: the blacksmith of the gods, whose face would be blackened from his forge's fire (*Antonio's would have been blackened from gunpowder*) |
| 52-58 | 'He was the captain of some trifling little ship, not worth the effort of capturing because it was so small. Yet this ship of his, by fighting us at close quarters, inflicted so much damage on our very best ships, that even we, his enemies, who had lost our ships because of him, were full of his praise. What |

|        | one of my friends. |
| Duke   | Thou shalt not be the worse for me. There's gold. |
| Feste  | But that it would be double-dealing, sir, I would you could make it another. |
| Duke   | O, you give me ill counsel. |
| Feste  | Put your grace in your pocket, sir, for this once, 30 and let your flesh and blood obey it. |
| Duke   | Well, I will be so much a sinner to be a double dealer; there's another. |
| Feste  | Primo, secundo, tertio, is a good play, and the old saying is, 'the third pays for all'; the triplex, sir, is a good tripping measure, or the bells of Saint Bennet, sir, may put you in mind—one, two, three. |
| Duke   | You can fool no more money out of me at this throw. If you will let your lady know I am here 40 to speak with her and bring her along with you, it may awake my bounty further. |
| Feste  | Marry, sir, lullaby to your bounty till I come again. I go, sir, but I would not have you to think that my desire of having is the sin of covetousness; but, as you say, sir, let your bounty take a nap; I will awake it anon. |

*Exit*

*Enter* Antonio *and* Officers

| Viola  | Here comes the man, sir, that did rescue me. |
| Duke   | That face of his I do remember well; Yet, when I saw it last, it was besmeared 50 As black as Vulcan in the smoke of war. A bawbling vessel was he captain of, For shallow draught and bulk unprizable, |

is he charged with?' (*Orsino has spoken spontaneously his admiration for Antonio's bravery, but now he has to act in his role of magistrate.*)

60–61    **fraught from Candy:** cargo on its way from Crete

64    **desperate . . . state:** 'careless of decent law-abiding behaviour'

65    **apprehend:** arrest (*Antonio was a wanted man, but he was also breaking the law when he was caught.*)

66–68    'He was most kind to me and drew his sword to defend me; but afterwards I couldn't make head or tail of what he was saying to me. I can only think it was some kind of madness.' (*Viola has already told Orsino how she was rescued from Sir Toby's attack, and now she is quick to speak up on Antonio's behalf.*)

69    **Notable:** notorious

   **salt-water thief:** *not some little river pirate, but one operating on the high seas*

72    **in terms . . . dear:** by such violent and crippling means

74–96    'My lord, let me clear myself of those names you called me; I have never been a thief or a pirate, though I agree that I was your enemy, but not without good cause. I was drawn to this place by a kind of witchcraft. That ungrateful boy there, standing next to you, I saved from the gaping jaws of the wild hungry sea. He was a piece of human wreckage that couldn't possibly have survived. Well, I gave him back his life, and, in addition gave him my love unstintingly, devoting myself to him. It was for his sake, purely out of love for him, that I risked my life by coming into this dangerous enemy town. When I found him being attacked I drew my sword to protect him; then when I was arrested he was so disloyally cautious about making sure he didn't share my danger, that he had the cheek to tell me to my face that he did not know me; in the twinkling of an eye he grew as distant as though we hadn't seen each other for 20 years; he even refused to give me back my purse which I had entrusted to him not half an hour before.' (*Antonio can only explain his being so deceived into devoted friendship with Sebastian by saying he was under a spell. He is the first to point an accusing finger at Viola. Gradually she becomes ringed about with people demanding an explanation.*)

|            | With which such scathful grapple did he make |
|------------|-----------------------------------------------|
|            | With the most noble bottom of our fleet, |
|            | That very envy and the tongue of loss |
|            | Cried fame and honour on him. What's the |
|            | matter? |
| 1 Off.     | Orsino, this is that Antonio |
|            | That took the *Phœnix* and her fraught from     60 |
|            | Candy, |
|            | And this is he that did the *Tiger* board, |
|            | When your young nephew, Titus, lost his leg. |
|            | Here in the streets, desperate of shame and state, |
|            | In private brabble did we apprehend him. |
| Viola      | He did me kindness, sir, drew on my side, |
|            | But in conclusion put strange speech upon me; |
|            | I know not what 'twas but distraction. |
| Duke       | Notable pirate, thou salt-water thief! |
|            | What foolish boldness brought thee to their     70 |
|            | mercies, |
|            | Whom thou in terms so bloody and so dear |
|            | Hast made thine enemies? |
| Antonio    | Orsino, noble sir, |
|            | Be pleased that I shake off these names you |
|            | give me; |
|            | Antonio never yet was thief or pirate, |
|            | Though I confess, on base and ground enough, |
|            | Orsino's enemy. A witchcraft drew me hither. |
|            | That most ungrateful boy there by your side     80 |
|            | From the rude sea's enraged and foamy mouth |
|            | Did I redeem—a wreck past hope he was. |
|            | His life I gave him, and did thereto add |
|            | My love, without retention or restraint, |
|            | All his in dedication. For his sake |
|            | Did I expose myself—pure for his love— |

| 100–101 | 'Not for a single minute were we parted.' |
| 102 | *Again, Viola does not have a chance to cross-examine Antonio. The bewilderment must be protracted as long as possible. With Olivia's arrival, Orsino's mind passes to more important matters.* |
| 103 | *Orsino marvels to himself as his goddess approaches.* |
| 104 | **But for thee, fellow:** 'As far as you are concerned, Antonio' |
| 108–109 | 'What do you want apart from the one thing you cannot have? Name it, and I shall see whether I am able to serve you.' (*Now that she cannot marry Orsino, Olivia can afford to seem generous.*) |
| 113 | *Olivia silences Orsino so that she can speak to Cesario, whom she is surprised to see still in service with Orsino.* |
| 115 | 'If it is the same old story' |
| 116 | **fat and fulsome:** sickening and unnecessary (*like having too much food*) |

|         | Into the danger of this adverse town; |
|---------|---------------------------------------|
|         | Drew to defend him when he was beset; |
|         | Where, being apprehended, his false cunning, |
|         | Not meaning to partake with me in danger, |
|         | Taught him to face me out of his acquaintance, |
|         | And grew a twenty years removed thing |
|         | While one would wink; denied me mine own purse, |
|         | Which I had recommended to his use |
|         | Not half an hour before. |
| Viola   | How can this be? |
| Duke    | When came he to this town? |
| Antonio | Today, my lord. And for three months before, |
|         | No interim, not a minute's vacancy, |
|         | Both day and night did we keep company. |

*Enter* Olivia *and attendants*

| Duke   | Here comes the countess. |
|--------|--------------------------|
|        | Now heaven walks on earth! |
|        | But for thee, fellow—fellow, thy words are madness; |
|        | Three months this youth hath tended upon me— |
|        | But more of that anon. Take him aside. |
| Olivia | What would my lord, but that he may not have, |
|        | Wherein Olivia may seem serviceable? |
|        | Cesario, you do not keep promise with me. |
| Viola  | Madam! |
| Duke   | Gracious Olivia— |
| Olivia | What do you say, Cesario? Good my lord— |
| Viola  | My lord would speak, my duty hushes me. |
| Olivia | If it be aught to the old tune, my lord, |
|        | It is as fat and fulsome to mine ear |

119    **constant:** *one of the last words one would apply to Olivia—though she has been constant in rejecting Orsino*

120–124    'Are you still set in your obstinacy? What a cruel lady you are! Here have I been offering up the most faithful and devoted love to that thankless heart of yours which holds out no hope to me.' (*Orsino uses similar language to Antonio's. They have put Olivia and Sebastian respectively on a pedestal. Now it is Orsino's turn to find how far his picture of Olivia and his imagined love for her is from the truth.*)

125–126    'Do just whatever you like, my lord.'

128    **the Egyptian thief:** *An old story told how the robber Thyamis, when his hide-out was surrounded, decided to kill his lover before his enemies seized her. Orsino feels the need to do something violent: even the idea of killing Olivia because he cannot have her occurs to him as a possible, sufficiently melodramatic gesture.*

130    **savours nobly:** has a touch of greatness

131–141    'Just listen to me. Since you think nothing about my devotion and since I have more than a suspicion (*said with a glance at Cesario*) who is the person forcing me from the place I should occupy in your heart (*Orsino does not doubt for a minute that he deserves Olivia's love*), then I'll leave you to it—go on being your cold cruel self! But as for this darling of yours, whom I know you love, and for whom, I must admit, I have a strong affection, I will snatch him away from your sight where he seems to have installed himself triumphing over his master.' (*This is the first time Orsino has openly admitted his affection for Cesario. It helps us to believe in his eventual acceptance of Viola as a replacement for Olivia.*)

144    **the lamb:** *Cesario*

144–145    *Orsino is threatening to kill Cesario to spite Olivia who, for all her gentle innocent air—like a* 'dove'—*is really black-hearted—like a* 'raven'.

146    **jocund, apt:** gladly and readily

147    **To do you rest:** To set your mind at rest (*Orsino and Viola both act melodramatically; Orsino blinded by annoyance and Viola by love.*)

149    *At last Viola confesses her love for Orsino, but Orsino has already turned away, and Olivia still believes it is a page's hero-worship of his master. Viola still has the presence of mind to remember that she is supposed to be a man.*

As howling after music.

**Duke**     Still so cruel?

**Olivia**     Still so constant, lord.

**Duke**     What, to perverseness? You uncivil lady,     120
To whose ingrate and unauspicious altars
My soul the faithfullest offerings hath breathed
out
That e'er devotion tendered! What shall I do?

**Olivia**     Even what it please my lord, that shall become
him.

**Duke**     Why should I not, had I the heart to do it,
Like to the Egyptian thief at point of death,
Kill what I love? A savage jealousy,
That sometime savours nobly!     130
    But hear me this:
Since you to non-regardance cast my faith,
And that I partly know the instrument
That screws me from my true place in your
favour,
Live you the marble-breasted tyrant still.
But this your minion—whom I know you love,
And whom, by heaven I swear, I tender
dearly—
Him will I tear out of that cruel eye,     140
Where he sits crowned in his master's spite.
    Come, boy, with me; my thoughts are ripe in
mischief.
I'll sacrifice the lamb that I do love,
To spite a raven's heart within a dove.

**Viola**     And I most jocund, apt and willingly,
To do you rest a thousand deaths would die.

**Olivia**     Where goes Cesario?

**Viola**     After him I love

| | |
|---|---|
| 151 | **by all mores:** more than anything you care to mention |
| 152–153 | 'If that's not the truth, may heaven punish me for soiling my love by lying about it.' |
| 154 | **detested:** 'Am I being rejected then?' |
| 157 | **forgot thyself:** forgotten that you are my husband |
| | **so long:** *since they exchanged their oaths* |
| 160–163 | *The word* 'husband' *shoots back and forth four times like a shuttlecock, and brings Orsino striding back into the centre of the scene.* |
| 165–169 | 'It is only cowardly fear that silences you from revealing who you are now. Don't be afraid, Cesario; accept your fortune; show yourself the man you know you now are, and then you will be equal in rank to the man you so fear.' (*As Olivia's lord and master, Cesario will be equal in rank to Orsino. Olivia can only think it is fear of Orsino that keeps Cesario from speaking up.*) |
| 171–175 | 'Father, by your responsibility as a priest, I command you now to reveal what you know has just a short while ago been transacted between this young man and myself—even though we had just been planning to keep secret what we are now forced to tell everyone before we are ready.' |
| 176–184 | *The priest bears witness solemnly in one long formal sentence. Each heavy phrase seems to force home the permanence of the bond of marriage; each is a further blow to Orsino.* |
| 177 | **mutual joinder of:** both joining |
| 178 | 'pledged with a formal kiss' |

|          | More than I love these eyes, more than my life, 150 |
|          | More, by all mores, than e'er I shall love wife. |
|          | If I do feign, you witnesses above |
|          | Punish my life for tainting of my love. |
| Olivia   | Ay me, detested! How am I beguiled! |
| Viola    | Who does beguile you? Who does do you wrong? |
| Olivia   | Hast thou forgot thyself? Is it so long? |
|          | Call forth the holy father. |
| Duke     | Come, away! |
| Olivia   | Whither, my lord? Cesario, husband, stay. 160 |
| Duke     | Husband? |
| Olivia   | Ay, husband. Can he that deny? |
| Duke     | Her husband, sirrah? |
| Viola    | No, my lord, not I. |
| Olivia   | Alas, it is the baseness of thy fear |
|          | That makes thee strangle thy propriety. |
|          | Fear not, Cesario, take thy fortunes up, |
|          | Be that thou knowest thou art, and then thou art |
|          | As great as that thou fearest. |

*Enter* Priest

|          | O welcome, father! 170 |
|          | Father, I charge thee by thy reverence |
|          | Here to unfold—though lately we intended |
|          | To keep in darkness what occasion now |
|          | Reveals before 'tis ripe—what thou dost know |
|          | Hath newly passed between this youth and me. |
| Priest   | A contract of eternal bond of love, |
|          | Confirmed by mutual joinder of your hands, |
|          | Attested by the holy close of lips, |
|          | Strengthened by interchangement of your rings, |

181      'sealed and witnessed by me in my capacity as a priest'

182–184      *A sober way of showing Orsino how recently Cesario has apparently deceived him.*

185–188      'You treacherous little fox! What are you going to be like when your skin starts sprouting grey hairs? Or, what is more likely—you'll get so cunning, that while you are tripping somebody up, you will trip yourself (and so be killed). *(Orsino's fury cannot now work itself out by killing anyone, so he chooses the most unpleasant vocabulary he can think of: 'grizzle'= beard; 'case'=face.)*

193      **Hold little faith:** Retain a little honour

194      *Orsino has once again turned on his heel, but remains to hear the third and least serious complaint against Cesario. The tension is neatly relieved by Sir Andrew's laments as he clutches his bleeding head, and then by Sir Toby's drunken unpleasantness.*

194      **presently:** at once

198      **coxcomb:** head *(like a cock's red tousled comb, matted with blood)*

199      *Sir Andrew has kept threatening to go home. Now he would give anything to be safely away from this mad-house.*

204      **incardinate:** *Sir Andrew's mistake for 'incarnate'—meaning 'in person'.*

206      *The stage is so crowded that Sir Andrew, like Sebastian in a minute, does not notice Cesario at first.*

206      **'Od's lifelings:** *literally* 'God's little lives' *(a weak enough oath for Sir Andrew to use, as he almost whines before Cesario. He has the coward's way of blaming someone else.)*

207      **set on:** encouraged

|          | And all the ceremony of this compact                  180 |
|          | Sealed in my function, by my testimony; |
|          | Since when, my watch hath told me, toward my grave |
|          | I have travelled but two hours. |
| Duke     | O thou dissembling cub! What wilt thou be |
|          | When time hath sowed a grizzle on thy case? |
|          | Or will not else thy craft so quickly grow, |
|          | That thine own trip shall be thine overthrow! |
|          | Farewell, and take her, but direct thy feet |
|          | Where thou and I henceforth may never meet.    190 |
| Viola    | My lord, I do protest— |
| Olivia   | O do not swear; |
|          | Hold little faith though thou hast too much fear. |

*Enter* Sir Andrew

| Andrew | For the love of God, a surgeon! Send one presently to Sir Toby. |
| Olivia | What's the matter? |
| Andrew | He's broke my head across, and he's given Sir Toby a bloody coxcomb too. For the love of God, your help! I had rather than forty pound I were at home.    200 |
| Olivia | Who has done this, Sir Andrew? |
| Andrew | The Count's gentleman, one Cesario; we took him for a coward, but he's the very devil incardinate. |
| Duke | My gentleman Cesario? |
| Andrew | 'Od's lifelings, here he is! You broke my head for nothing, and that that I did, I was set on to do it by Sir Toby. |
| Viola | Why do you speak to me? I never hurt you. |

211    **bespake you fair:** spoke politely to you

213    **set nothing by:** consider it nothing to have given me

214    **halting:** stumbling drunkenly

214–215    **you shall hear more:** *Sir Andrew expects a great outburst from Sir Toby, but he is, in fact, too drunk to care. The audience's last view of Sir Toby is of him at his least attractive. There is no danger of sympathy slipping away from Viola at this moment.*

216    **tickled you othergates:** set about you differently (*Sir Andrew is still loyal to Sir Toby and believes he would have beaten 'Cesario' previously if he had not been already half-drunk.*)

218    **That's all one:** 'What does it matter now?' (*Sir Toby's rude reply is the more striking by contrast to Orsino's polite concern.*)

219    **Sot:** fool (*Sir Toby assumes Feste is drunk too, as he leans heavily on him; Feste pretends to lurch drunkenly under the weight.*)

220    **agone:** ago

221    **set:** glazed; in a drunken stupor

222    **passy-measures pavin:** *an English version of a slow stately Italian pavane. In Sir Toby's mind the phrase* 'set at eight' *strikes a bell, and he thinks of this dance, which had eight bars to a phrase and so was* 'set at eight'. *The doctor will be equally slow in reaching this patient.*

226    **be dressed:** have our wounds bound up

229    **thin faced:** *a sneer at the meaning of Sir Andrew's surname*
    **gull:** fool (*Sir Toby has now nothing to gain from humouring Sir Andrew, who now has no chance of marrying Olivia, and he pours out his full scorn for his pitiable 'friend'.*)

231    *Olivia is the only person on stage that Sebastian at once recognises, and he is courteously apologetic to her. The return to verse form prepares for what is bound to be an emotional reuniting of brother and sister.*

233    **with wit and safety:** 'as it was the only sensible thing to do to protect myself'

234    **throw . . . regard:** stare oddly (*Sebastian has clearly accepted that Olivia is not mad and he thinks of the one probable reason for her strange manner.*)

237–238    'Pardon me, dear, if only because of the vows we took so recently.'

|          | You drew your sword upon me without cause,          210 |
|----------|-----------------------------------------------------|
|          | But I bespake you fair and hurt you not.            |
| Andrew   | If a bloody coxcomb be a hurt, you have hurt me;    |
|          | I think you set nothing by a bloody coxcomb.        |

*Enter* Sir Toby *and* Feste

|          | Here comes Sir Toby halting; you shall hear more; but if he had not been in drink, he would have tickled you othergates than he did. |
|----------|-----------------------------------------------------|
| Duke     | How now, gentleman! How is it with you?             |
| Toby     | That's all one. He's hurt me, and there's the end of it. Sot, didst see Dick Surgeon, sot? |
| Feste    | O, he's drunk, Sir Toby, an hour agone; his eyes 220 were set at eight in the morning. |
| Toby     | Then he's a rogue, and a passy-measures pavin! I hate a drunken rogue! |
| Olivia   | Away with him! Who hath made this havoc with them? |
| Andrew   | I'll help you, Sir Toby, because we'll be dressed together. |
| Toby     | Will you help? An ass-head and a coxcomb and a knave—a thin faced knave, a gull! |
| Olivia   | Get him to bed, and let his hurt be looked to.    230 |

*Exeunt* Feste, Sir Toby *and* Sir Andrew

*Enter* Sebastian

| Sebas.   | I am sorry, madam, I have hurt your kinsman;      |
|----------|---------------------------------------------------|
|          | But had it been the brother of my blood,          |
|          | I must have done no less with wit and safety.     |
|          | You throw a strange regard upon me, and by that   |
|          | I do perceive it hath offended you.               |
|          | Pardon me, sweet one, even for the vows           |

239     'Two people who look, speak and dress exactly the same'

240     **natural perspective:** an optical delusion created by nature
        (*Orsino's words said more to himself go unheeded by Sebastian who
        has just noticed his friend, Antonio. He is delighted to find him again,
        as his language shows.*)

242     **racked:** tortured (*as though his body was being broken on the
        rack*)

245     'How could you possibly doubt it, Antonio?'

249     *At last Olivia has found breath to speak what they all feel. She is the
        one most deeply affected by the mistake.*

251–252 'I'm sure I cannot be like a god, able to be in different places
        at the same time.'

253     **blind:** *to Viola's beauty which they were destroying*

255     **Of charity:** For pity's sake

260–262 'He was dressed exactly as you are when he was drowned. If
        evil spirits are able to adopt human shape and wear clothes,
        then you must be one come to frighten us.' (*Sebastian naturally
        hesitates to believe this is Viola because she is apparently a man.
        Viola does not immediately greet her brother because she fears that
        she is being deceived by some trick of the devil's.*)

263     **spirit:** *Sebastian agrees that he is a being of some sort—i.e., he is
        mortal.*

264–265 'I am wearing the body which I inherited at birth.'

266     **as the rest goes even:** as everything else corresponds

269–275 *Viola and Sebastian are almost comical in their search for details
        which will confirm what they both wish to believe. Shakespeare is
        parodying the sickly romantic endings of many contemporary plays.*

|  | We made each other but so late ago. |
|---|---|
| Duke | One face, one voice, one habit, and two persons— |
|  | A natural perspective, that is and is not! 240 |
| Sebas. | Antonio! O, my dear Antonio! |
|  | How have the hours racked and tortured me, |
|  | Since I have lost thee! |
| Antonio | Sebastian are you? |
| Sebas. | Fearest thou that, Antonio? |
| Antonio | How have you made division of yourself? |
|  | An apple cleft in two is not more twin |
|  | Than these two creatures. Which is Sebastian? |
| Olivia | Most wonderful! |
| Sebas. | Do I stand there? I never had a brother; 250 |
|  | Nor can there be that deity in my nature |
|  | Of here and everywhere. I had a sister, |
|  | Whom the blind waves and surges have |
|  | devoured. |
|  | Of charity, what kin are you to me? |
|  | What countryman? What name? What |
|  | parentage? |
| Viola | Of Messaline. Sebastian was my father. |
|  | Such a Sebastian was my brother too; |
|  | So went he suited to his watery tomb. 260 |
|  | If spirits can assume both form and suit, |
|  | You come to fright us. |
| Sebas. | A spirit I am indeed; |
|  | But am in that dimension grossly clad |
|  | Which from the womb I did participate. |
|  | Were you a woman, as the rest goes even, |
|  | I should my tears let fall upon your cheek, |
|  | And say, 'Thrice-welcome, drowned Viola!' |
| Viola | My father had a mole upon his brow— |

273–275   'I remember that clearly. He died on my sister's 13th birthday.'

276–286   'If the only thing that prevents us both from being happy is these men's clothes that I have no right to wear, then just wait to kiss me until everything comes to fit together exactly to prove that I really am Viola. To prove this, I'll take you to meet a certain captain in this town with whom I left my girl's clothes. It was with his kindly help that I was recommended to this count's service. Everything I have done since has been connected with the affairs of this lady, Olivia, and this count, Orsino.' (*The conversation is brought neatly back to Olivia and Orsino.*)

287   **mistook:** accidentally deceived

288   'By letting you be deceived nature was just following her mysteriously wise course.' (*Like a bowl swerving with the weighted bias on to its true course; here nature has aimed Olivia to meet Sebastian in a roundabout way.*)

289   **contracted:** engaged

291   **maid:** *a pun, because a* 'maid' *also meant* a man who had had no previous lover (*Sebastian jokingly shows Olivia how by marrying him she is doing the apparently impossible—marrying both a maid and a man.*)

293   **the glass seems true:** 'what looked like an optical delusion seems, after all, to be real' (*and there really are two people standing here*)

294   **happy wreck:** 'shipwreck which has ended happily' (*Orsino is also quick to salvage something from the shipwreck of his hopes of marrying Olivia. The speed with which he now switches his affection to Viola comically deflates his pose as a rejected lover with a broken heart.*)

296   **like to me:** in the same way as you cared for me

297–300   'And everything I once said I will swear to again, and I will keep to my word as faithfully as the heavens keep the sun in the sky.'

| | | |
|---|---|---|
| Sebas. | And so had mine. | 270 |

Viola    And died that day when Viola from her birth
Had numbered thirteen years—

Sebas.    O, that record is lively in my soul!
He finished indeed his mortal act
That day that made my sister thirteen years.

Viola    If nothing lets to make us happy both,
But this my masculine usurped attire,
Do not embrace me till each circumstance
Of place, time, fortune, do cohere and jump
That I am Viola; which to confirm,     280
I'll bring you to a captain in this town
Where lie my maiden weeds; by whose gentle help,
I was preferred to serve this noble count.
All the occurrence of my fortune since
Hath been between this lady and this lord.

Sebas.    So comes it, lady, you have been mistook;
But nature to her bias drew in that.
You would have been contracted to a maid,
Nor are you therein, by my life, deceived;     290
You are betrothed both to a maid and man.

Duke    Be not amazed; right noble is his blood.
    If this be so, as yet the glass seems true,
I shall have share in this most happy wreck.
Boy, thou hast said to me a thousand times
Thou never shouldst love woman like to me.

Viola    And all those sayings will I over-swear,
And all those swearings keep as true in soul,
As doth that orbed continent, the fire
That severs day from night.     300

Duke    Give me thy hand,
And let me see thee in thy woman's weeds.

| | |
|---|---|
| 304–305 | **He upon . . . suit:** 'As a result of some lawsuit, Malvolio has had him put under arrest' (*What the Captain has done wrong is never explained; but it reminds Olivia of the one piece of the jigsaw not yet put into place—Malvolio.*) |
| 307–311 | 'He shall set him free. Bring Malvolio here (*Olivia calls off-stage to a servant*); but now I remember someone told me that he had gone out of his mind. A form of madness that took complete possession of me made me forget all about his madness.' (*Olivia has all the time realised that her infatuation for Cesario is a kind of madness.*) |
| 313–318 | 'Truly, my lady, he wards off the devil as well as anyone in his mad condition. I have a letter here he wrote to you. You ought to have had it this morning, but, since letters from a madman needn't be thought of as the gospel truth, it doesn't matter very much when they are delivered.' (*Feste is playfully punning on the names of the books in the New Testament.*) |
| 313 | **stave:** a long stick used in duelling |
| 320–321 | 'You can expect to learn a lot from a clown reading out a madman's words!' (*Feste is jokingly sarcastic, and then launches into the supposed voice of a madman to read out the letter.*) |
| 324–326 | 'I'm only reading the words of a madman. If your ladyship wishes to hear it properly, you must let me read it in the appropriate voice.' |
| 328 | **his right wits:** properly (*and so proper to a madman*) |
| 329 | **perpend:** attention, everyone (*Feste has just drawn breath to continue the letter in the same mad voice, thinking he has proved his point, when Olivia interrupts. She has less patience now for such clowning and wants the matter settled quickly.*) |

| | |
|---|---|
| Viola | The captain that did bring me first on shore<br>Hath my maid's garments. He upon some action<br>Is now in durance at Malvolio's suit,<br>A gentleman and follower of my lady's. |
| Olivia | He shall enlarge him. Fetch Malvolio hither.<br>And yet, alas, now I remember me;<br>They say, poor gentleman, he's much distract.<br>A most extracting frenzy of mine own     310<br>From my remembrance clearly banished his. |

*Enter* Feste *with a letter*

| | |
|---|---|
| | How does he, sirrah? |
| Feste | Truly, madam, he holds Beelzebub at the stave's end as well as a man in his case may do. He's here writ a letter to you. I should have given it you today morning. But as a madman's epistles are no gospels, so it skills not much when they are delivered. |
| Olivia | Open it, and read it. |
| Feste | Look then to be well edified, when the fool de-  320 livers the madman.<br>*(in a mad voice) By the Lord, madam—* |
| Olivia | How now, art thou mad? |
| Feste | No madam, I do but read madness; an your ladyship will have it as it ought to be, you must allow Vox. |
| Olivia | Prithee, read in thy right wits. |
| Feste | So I do, madonna; but to read his right wits is to read thus. Therefore perpend, my princess, and give ear.     330 |
| Olivia | *(to* Fabian) Read it you, sirrah. |
| Fabian | *(reads) By the Lord, madam, you wrong me, and the* |

335–340     **yet have ... injury:** 'yet I am as sane as you are, my lady.
I have your very letter which urged me to behave as strangely
as I did, and I am sure it will prove either that I was in the
right, or that you have behaved shamefully. You may think
what you like about me. I may have been rather outspoken
for one in my position, but I have just been allowing my
wrongs to speak for themselves.' (*The letter shows that Malvolio
has at last stopped thinking Olivia is in love with him. His anger at
being tricked by her bursts through the formal expressions a steward
might use in writing to his mistress.*)

341     **Madly-used:** *He has been not just badly-used, but treated as
though he were mad.*

344     'It doesn't sound much like madness.'

346–351     'My lord, now that you have had a chance to take in all that
has happened, if you could bring yourself to accept me as a
sister as eagerly as you thought of me as your future wife,
then the same day could see us all joined in marriage, with
the ceremony here at my house and at my own expense.'
(*Olivia is tactfully trying to make peace with Orsino, who has had
time to adjust himself to the new idea of marrying Viola, while
Malvolio's letter was being read.*)

352     'Madam, I most willingly accept your offer.'

353     **Your ... you:** 'I now release you from my service.' (*Orsino has
recovered his poise and is once more the gracious lord.*)

355     **mettle:** nature (*Viola has had a hard passage in her role of
Cesario.*)

356     *Orsino is very much aware that he is now addressing a lady of equal
rank with Olivia. To have become his servant, Viola must have set
aside her dignity.*

358–359     *Orsino's elegant way of proposing to Viola.*

360     *Olivia is delighted to embrace Viola and welcome her as a sister-in-law.*

world shall know it. Though you have put me into darkness, and given your drunken cousin rule over me, yet have I the benefit of my senses as well as your ladyship. I have your own letter that induced me to the semblance I put on; with the which I doubt not but to do myself much right, or you much shame. Think of me as you please. I leave my duty a little unthought of, and speak out of my injury.                                                    340

*The Madly-used Malvolio.*

| | |
|---|---|
| Olivia | Did he write this? |
| Feste | Ay, madam. |
| Duke | This savours not much of distraction. |
| Olivia | See him delivered, Fabian; bring him hither. |

*Exit* Fabian

My lord, so please you, these things further thought on,
To think me as well a sister as a wife,
One day shall crown the alliance of it, so please you,                                                    350
Here at my house and at my proper cost.

Duke    I am most apt to embrace your offer.
(*to* Viola) Your master quits you; and,
for your service done him,
So much against the mettle of your sex,
So far beneath your soft and tender breeding,
And since you called me master for so long,
Here is my hand; you shall from this time be
Your master's mistress.

Olivia    A sister! You are she.                                                    360

*Enter* Malvolio *and* Fabian

Duke    Is this the madman?

364     **Notorious:** disgraceful (*Quivering with rage, Malvolio points an accusing finger at Olivia. We can't help but sympathise with him at this moment—he seems to have much more to complain of than Sir Toby and Sir Andrew. Yet if he rouses too much sympathy, the play will leave a sour taste. He is still comical in his offended dignity, and an Elizabethan audience would be delighted at this parody of the pompously important Controller of the Queen's household, Sir William Knowles.*)

366     *Malvolio challenges Olivia to prove there and then that her hand-writing and style are different from the letter he thrusts at Olivia.*

366–382     'Yes, Madam, you have. I beg you to read that letter—you cannot deny that it is in your writing. I challenge you to write differently, if you can—either in hand-writing or with different phrasing. Deny it's your seal (*Maria had 'borrowed' Olivia's signet-ring to seal the letter*) or composed by you. Of course you can't.

    'Very well then, admit it is your letter, and tell me—if you can, without robbing yourself of all traces of respect we may have for you—why you gave me such obvious signs of love, why you ordered me to come in smiling and wearing cross-gartering and yellow stockings and to scorn Sir Toby and the less important servants; and why when I obeyed these instructions, fully expecting you to reward me, you allowed me to be shut away, locked in a darkened room, visited by a parson, and turned into the most duped idiot that was ever made fool of by man's wit. Go on, tell me.'

383–396     'I'm sorry, Malvolio, but this is not written by me—though I agree that the handwriting is very like mine. Undoubtedly it is Maria's. Come to think of it—she was the one who first told me you were mad. Then you came in pulling your face into smiles, acting and dressed exactly in the way the letter suggested to you. But don't worry. I know this plot has certainly hit you hard; but when we've found out who were responsible and what their motives were, I'll let you conduct your own case against them and pass sentence on them.' (*Olivia starts to appreciate how subtle Maria was in preparing the ground for her plot. The threat of trial and punishment introduces a*

| | |
|---|---|
| Olivia | Ay, my lord, this same. How now, Malvolio? |
| Malv. | Madam, you have done me wrong,<br>Notorious wrong. |
| Olivia | Have I, Malvolio? No! |
| Malv. | Lady, you have. Pray you, peruse that letter.<br>You must not now deny it is your hand;<br>Write from it, if you can, in hand or phrase,<br>Or say 'tis not your seal, not your invention—<br>You can say none of this. |
| | Well, grant it then,<br>And tell me, in the modesty of honour,<br>When you have given me such clear lights of<br>favour,<br>Bade me come smiling and cross-gartered to you,<br>To put on yellow stockings, and to frown<br>Upon Sir Toby and the lighter people;<br>And, acting this in an obedient hope,<br>Why have you suffered me to be imprisoned,<br>Kept in a dark house, visited by the priest,<br>And made the most notorious geck and gull,<br>That e'er invention played on? Tell me why. |
| Olivia | Alas, Malvolio, this is not my writing,<br>Though I confess much like the character;<br>But, out of question, 'tis Maria's hand.<br>And, now I do bethink me, it was she<br>First told me thou wast mad; then camest in<br>smiling,<br>And in such forms which here were presupposed<br>Upon thee in the letter. Prithee, be content;<br>This practice hath most shrewdly passed upon<br>thee.<br>But, when we know the grounds and authors<br>of it,<br>Thou shalt be both the plaintiff and the judge |

370

380

390

*serious note which Fabian is quick to observe. He realises that it is better to confess than to be found out, and Olivia is in the right mood now to pardon them.*)

398–405   'Don't let any quarrel or future dispute spoil the happy atmosphere now which I have watched in amazement. In the hope that it won't, I openly confess that Toby and I played this trick upon Malvolio, because of the haughtiness and rudeness which we had noticed in him. Maria wrote the letter because Sir Toby insisted so strongly.' (*Fabian shelters Maria from blame, by saying that the plot was Sir Toby's and his invention.*)

406   *Such a marriage has been hinted at before; it is Maria's reward for using her wits.*

407–408   'What happened later as we teased him to get our own back will more likely make people want to laugh than want to punish us.'

409–410   *Fabian believes that their trick was fair enough—tit-for-tat.*

411   **poor fool:** *Olivia's tone is sympathetic, not scornful*
      **baffled:** deceived

412   *Feste was the first of the play's characters to be spurned by Malvolio; so it is appropriate that he is the last character to reveal how he has had his revenge. His three taunting quotations, uttered in the same tones Malvolio used on the three earlier occasions, are all that is necessary to make his point.*

414   **interlude:** little play

414–415   **that's all one:** it doesn't matter now

415–416   **But do you remember?:** *This is the moment Malvolio may perhaps have forgotten, but it has rankled in Feste's mind.*

418   'time, which is so unpredictable, has had its revenge.'
      **whirligig:** spinning top

419   *Malvolio sees only grinning faces round him and includes everyone in his parting threat. He is not the sort of person who could easily be soothed, and it would be inappropriate if he suddenly changed character just to fit in with the play's happy ending.*

421   **entreat him to a peace:** beg him to calm down (*Orsino does not share Olivia's concern; he is anxious only to see Viola a woman once more.*)

423   **golden . . . convents:** 'when a happy hour has been found suitable' (*for the two marriages*)

424   **combination:** joining together (*in matrimony*)

|          | Of thine own cause. |
|----------|---------------------|
| Fabian   | Good madam, hear me speak, |
|          | And let no quarrel nor no brawl to come |
|          | Taint the condition of this present hour, |
|          | Which I have wondered at. In hope it shall not    400 |
|          | Most freely I confess; myself and Toby |
|          | Set this device against Malvolio here, |
|          | Upon some stubborn and uncourteous parts |
|          | We had conceived in him. Maria writ |
|          | The letter at Sir Toby's great importance, |
|          | In recompense whereof he hath married her. |
|          | How with a sportful malice it was followed |
|          | May rather pluck on laughter than revenge, |
|          | If that the injuries be justly weighed |
|          | That have on both sides passed.                   410 |
| Olivia   | Alas, poor fool, how have they baffled thee! |
| Feste    | Why, *Some are born great, some achieve greatness, and some have greatness thrown upon them.* I was one, sir, in this interlude; one Sir Topas, sir—but that's all one. *By the Lord, fool, I am not mad.* But do you remember? *Madam, why laugh you at such a barren rascal? An you smile not, he's gagged!* And thus the whirligig of time brings in his revenges. |
| Malv.    | I'll be revenged on the whole pack of you! |

*Exit*

| Olivia   | He hath been most notoriously abused.             420 |
|----------|-------------------------------------------------------|
| Duke     | Pursue him, and entreat him to a peace. |
|          | He hath not told us of the captain yet; |
|          | When that is known, and golden time convents, |
|          | A solemn combination shall be made |

425 **sweet sister:** *Orsino shows he has forgiven Olivia and can now think of her as a sister.*

427 **so:** *i.e., called by a man's name*

428 **habits:** clothes

429 **fancy's:** love's (*Orsino's final words are an echo of his mood in the first scene, but his tone shows that this mood is likely to be more lasting.*)

430 *Just as it appears that Orsino has delivered the play's last words, the audience notices Feste left alone on the stage. A song is a fit ending to a play which began with a group of court musicians, and burst from time to time into song and laughter. Yet Feste's song is not a marriage hymn, as might have been expected, nor even about lovers. This time he is not commissioned to sing by a patron, and so he chooses a simple story of a very ordinary man's progress through life, while the wind blows and rain patters down indifferent to man's actions. Many of the play's characters have tried to blind themselves to reality and have discovered their folly. This song does not make the same mistake.*

430 **and a:** but a

432 'When I did something wrong it was put down as childishness'

436–437 'No one would have anything to do with a rogue like me'

439 **wive:** marry

441 'It was no good trying to bluster my way through life'

443 'When I was so incapacitated that I had to be put to bed'

445 'I was always getting dead drunk with my drinking mates'

449 **But that's all one:** 'What does it all matter?'

450 *Feste humbly bows the play to its end with a conventional phrase, asking for the audience's applause.*

Of our dear souls. Meantime, sweet sister,
We will not part from hence. Cesario, come—
For so you shall be while you are a man—
But when in other habits you are seen,
Orsino's mistress, and his fancy's queen.

*Exeunt all but* Feste

Feste      (*sings*):

When that I was and a little tiny boy,      430
  With hey, ho, the wind and the rain;
A foolish thing was but a toy,
  For the rain it raineth every day.

But when I came to man's estate,
  With hey, ho, the wind and the rain;
'Gainst knaves and thieves men shut their
    gate,
  For the rain it raineth every day.

But when I came alas to wive,
  With hey, ho, the wind and the rain;      440
By swaggering could I never thrive,
  For the rain it raineth every day.

But when I came unto my beds,
  With hey, ho, the wind and the rain;
With toss-pots still had drunken heads,
  For the rain it raineth every day.

A great while ago the world began,
  With hey, ho, the wind and the rain;
But that's all one, our play is done,
  And we'll strive to please you every day.    450

*Exit*

# The plays in the Montague Shakespeare series